THE

NORTON SCORES

An Anthology for Listening

Standard Edition, Revised

THE

NORTON SCORES

An Anthology for Listening

STANDARD EDITION, REVISED

EDITED BY

ROGER KAMIEN

ASSISTANT PROFESSOR OF MUSIC, QUEENS COLLEGE
OF THE CITY UNIVERSITY OF NEW YORK

W · W · NORTON & COMPANY · INC ·
New York

Acknowledgments

The scores for items 1, 3, and 4 are reprinted from *Master-pieces of Music Before 1750*, edited by Carl Parrjsh and John F. Ohl, New York: W. W. Norton & Company, 1951.

The scores for items 10, 11, 13, 15, 16, 18, 20, 23, 24, 25, 31, 34, 36, and 37 are reprinted with the kind permission of Ernst Eulenburg Ltd., from the complete scores published in the Eulenberg miniature score series.

The scores for items 17, 30, 32, and 38 are reprinted by kind permission of G. Schirmer, Inc.

The scores for items 43, 46, and 48 are reprinted by kind permission of Boosey and Hawkes, Inc.

The score for item 41 is reprinted by kind permission of C. F. Peters Co.

The scores for items 42 and 47 are reprinted by kind permission of the Theodore Presser Company.

The translations for items 21, 22, 29, 33, and 39 are reprinted from *The Ring of Words*, edited by Philip L. Miller, by kind permission of Doubleday & Company, Inc.

ISBN 0 393 02167 8 (Cloth Edition)
ISBN 0 393 09386 7 (Paper Edition)

PRINTED IN THE UNITED STATES OF AMERICA

3 4 5 6 7 8 9 0

Contents

Preface

This anthology is designed for use in introductory music courses, where the ability to read music is not a prerequisite. The unique system of highlighting employed in this book enables students to follow full orchestral scores after about one hour of instruction. This system also has the advantage of permitting students who *can* read music to perceive every aspect of the score. It is felt that our system of highlighting will be of greater pedagogical value than artificially condensed scores, which restrict the student's vision to pre-selected elements of the music. The use of scores in introductory courses makes the student's listening experience more intense and meaningful, and permits the instructor to discuss music in greater depth.

The forty-eight works included in this Revised Edition have been chosen from among those most frequently studied in introductory courses. They range from the sixteenth century up to the middle of the twentieth, and represent a wide variety of forms, genres, and performing media. For the Revised Edition, it has been possible to expand the coverage of twentieth-century music. About half of the pieces are given in their entirety, while the others are represented by complete movements or sections that are particularly suitable for classroom study. Scenes from operas and some choral works are presented in vocal score, while all others are reprinted in their full original form. This anthology may be used together with any introductory text. A set of recordings is available from the publisher, containing forty-three of the selections.

A few words about the highlighting system employed in the full scores: Each system of score is covered with a light gray screen, and the most prominent line in the music at any given point is spotlighted by a white band (see No. 1 in sample on page x). In cases where two or more simultaneous lines are equally prominent, they are each highlighted. When a musical line continues from one system or page to the next, the white highlighting band ends with a wedge shape at the right-hand margin, and its continuation begins with a reverse wedge shape (see No. 2 in sample). By following these white bands in sequence through the score, the listener will perceive the notes corresponding to the most audible lines. Naturally, the highlighting will not *always* correspond with the most prominent instruments in a specific recording, for performances differ in their emphasis of particular lines. In such cases, we have highlighted those parts that, in our opinion, *should* emerge most clearly. To facilitate the following of highlighted scores, a narrow white band running the full width of the page has been placed between systems when there is more than one on a page.

It must be emphasized that we do not seek here to *analyze* melodic structure, contrapuntal texture, or any other aspect of the music. The highlighting may break off before the end of a phrase when the entrance of another part is more audible, and during long-held notes the attention will usually be drawn to more rhythmically active parts.

A few suggestions for the use of this anthology may be found useful:

1. The rudiments of musical notation should be introduced with a view to preparing the student to associate audible melodic contours with their written equivalents. It is more important for the beginning student to recognize rising and falling lines, and long and short notes, than to identify specific pitches or rhythms. It is helpful to explain the function of a tie, and the layout of a full score.

2. Before listening to a work, it is best for the student to familiarize himself with the names and abbreviations for instruments used in that particular score (a glossary of instrumental names and abbreviations will be found at the conclusion of the book). We have retained the Italian, German, French, and English names used in the scores reproduced in this anthology. This exposure to a wide range of terminology will prepare the student for later encounters with scores.

3. The student should be careful to notice whether there is more than one system on a page of score. He should be alerted for tempo changes, repeat signs, and *da capo* indications. Since performances often differ, it is helpful for the instructor to forewarn the class about the specific repeats made or not made in the recordings used for listening.

4. When a piece is very fast or difficult, it is helpful to listen once without a score.

5. It is best to begin with music that is relatively simple to follow: e.g. Schubert, *Heidenröslein;* Chopin, Prelude in E minor, Opus 28, No. 4, and Mazurka in B-flat major, Opus 7, No. 1; the second movement of Haydn's String Quartet in C major, Opus 76, No. 3; the two movements from Mozart's *Eine kleine Nachtmusik;* and the *Arabian Dance* from Tchaikovsky's *Nutcracker Suite.*

6. Important thematic material and passages that are difficult to follow

should be pointed out in advance and played either on the recording or at the piano. (We have found that rapid sections featuring two simultaneously highlighted instruments sometimes present difficulties for the student—e.g. Beethoven, Symphony No. 5, first movement, m. 65 ff., and Mozart, Symphony No. 40, first movement, m. 72 ff.)

We have attempted to keep the highlighted bands simple in shape while showing as much of the essential slurs and dynamic indication as possible. Occasionally, because of the layout of the original score, stray stems and slurs will intrude upon the white area and instrumental directions will be excluded from the highlighting. (Naturally, the beginning of a highlighted area will not always carry a dynamic or similar indication, as the indication may have occurred measures earlier when the instrument in question was not the most prominent.) As the student becomes more experienced in following the scores, he can be encouraged to direct his attention outside the highlighted areas, and with practice should eventually develop the skill to read conventional scores.

I should like to record here my great debt to the late Nathan Broder, who originated the system of highlighting employed here and whose advice and counsel were invaluable. My thanks go also to Mr. David Hamilton, who helped me avoid many errors. I am most grateful to my wife, Anita, who worked with me on every aspect of the book. She is truly the co-editor of this anthology.

R.K.

How to Follow the Highlighted Scores

1. The most prominent line in the music at any given time is highlighted by a white band.

2. When a musical line continues from one system (group of staffs) or page to the next, the white highlighted band ends with a wedge shape, and its continuation begins with a reverse wedge shape.

3. By following the highlighted bands in sequence through the score, the listener will perceive the notes corresponding to the most audible lines.

4. A narrow white band running the full width of the page separates one system from another when there is more than one on a page. It is very important to be alert for these separating bands.

5. When two or more lines are equally prominent, they are each highlighted. When encountering such passages for the first time, it is sometimes best to focus on only one of the lines.

THE

NORTON SCORES

An Anthology for Listening

Standard Edition, Revised

1. JOSQUIN DES PRÉS (c.1450-1521), *Ave Maria*

The chant *Ave Maria*

[Original a perfect fourth lower]

A - ve Ma - ri——a, gra - ti - a ple——na, Do - mi - nus te - cum,

be - ne - di - cta tu in—— mu - li——e - ri——bus, [etc.]

Translation

Hail, Mary, full of grace, the Lord is with thee; blessed art thou among women, and blessed the fruit of thy womb, Jesus Christ, Son of the living God. And blessed be thy breasts, that have suckled the King of Kings and the Lord our God.

2. GIOVANNI PIERLUIGI DA PALESTRINA (c.1525-1594), Kyrie from the *Pope Marcellus Mass* (PUBL. 1567)

Translation

Lord, have mercy upon us.
Christ, have mercy upon us.
Lord, have mercy upon us.

3. LUCA MARENZIO (1553-1599),
S'io parto, io moro (PUBL. 1594)

Note: The value of the quarter note remains constant in bars of varying lengths.

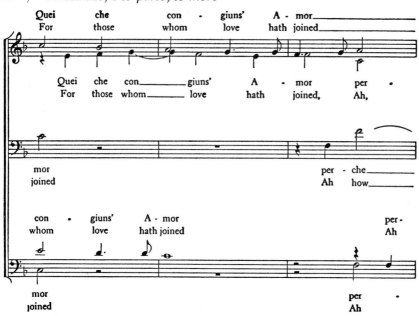

4. CLAUDIO MONTEVERDI (1567-1643),
Tu sei morta from *L'Orfeo* (1ST PERF. 1607)

Note: The value of the quarter note remains constant in bars of varying lengths.

cie - lo,   e   so - le,   ad - di   •   o.
hea - vens,   and sun - light,   for - e   •   ver.

5. ORLANDO GIBBONS (1583-1625),
The Silver Swan (PUBL. 1612)

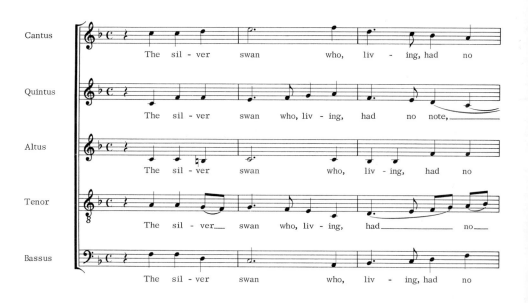

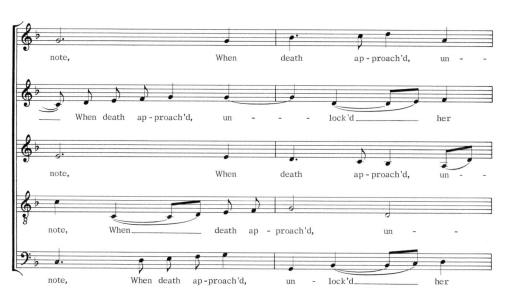

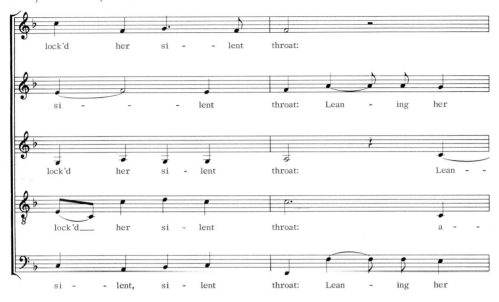

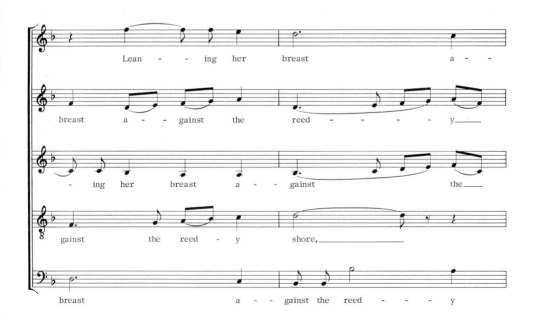

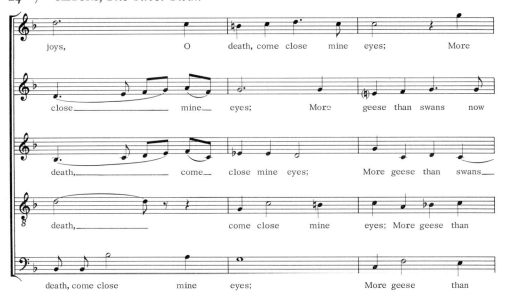

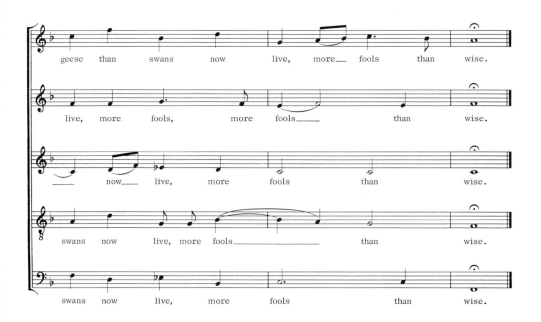

6. ARCANGELO CORELLI (1653-1713),
Sonata da chiesa, Opus 3, No. 7 (PUBL. 1689)

7. HENRY PURCELL (c.1659-1695), *Dido's Lament* from *Dido and Aeneas* (1ST PERF. 1689)

Thy hand, Bel - in - da! dark - - - ness shades me, On thy

bos - om let me rest, More I would, but death in -

vades me Death is now a wel - come guest!

When I am laid, am laid in

earth, may my wrongs cre - ate no trou - ble, no trou-ble in___ thy breast.

When I am laid,__ am laid_____ in earth, may my wrongs cre-

ate no trou-ble, no trou-ble in___ thy breast. Re - mem-ber me,

re - mem-ber me, But ah!_____ for-get my fate, Re -

8. GEORGE FRIDERIC HANDEL (1685-1759), Excerpts from *Messiah* (1741)

No. 2, Comfort Ye

— and the rough plac-es plain.

Ev-'ry val-ley,　　ev-'ry val-ley —

— shall be ex-alt - - - - - - - -

- - - - - - - - - ed,

No. 12, For unto us a Child is born

No. 23, He was despised

hair, and his cheeks to them that plucked off the

hair: He hid not His face from shame and

spit-ting, He hid not His face from shame,___

from shame,___ He hid not His

face from shame,_____ from shame and spitting.

D. C.

No. 44, Hallelujah

9. JOHANN SEBASTIAN BACH (1685-1750), Organ Fugue in G minor ("Little") (1709?)

10. BACH, Brandenburg Concerto No. 2 in F major (1721?)

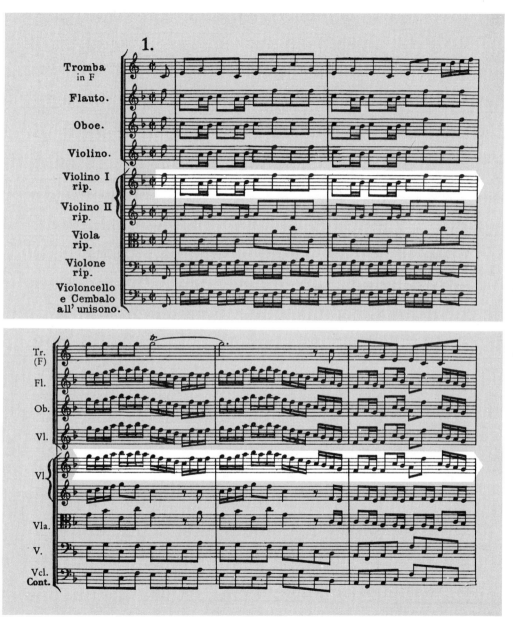

Ernst Eulenburg Ltd., London - Zürich

11. BACH, Air and Gigue from Suite No. 3 in D major (1723?)

Ernst Eulenburg Ltd., London - Zürich

12. BACH, Prelude and Fugue in C minor from
The Well-Tempered Clavier, Book I (PUBL. 1722)

13. BACH, Cantata No. 140, *Wachet auf* (1731)

Ernst Eulenburg Ltd.,
London · Zurich

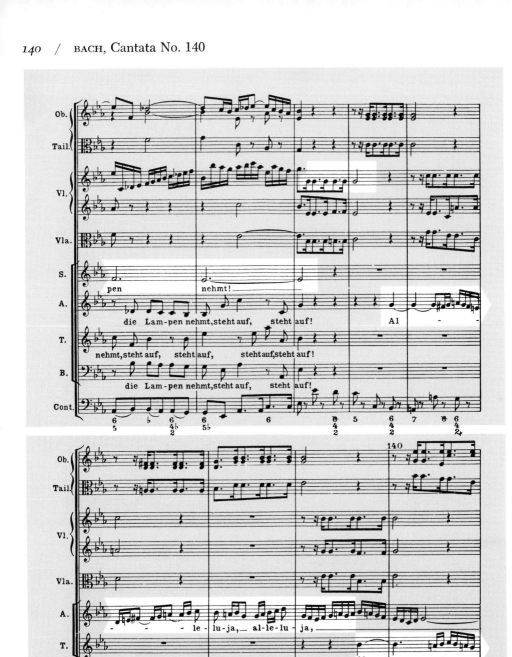

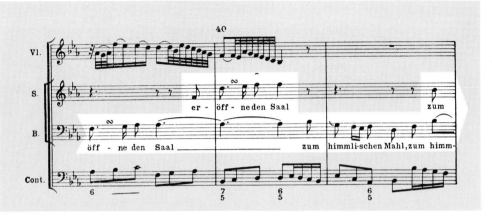

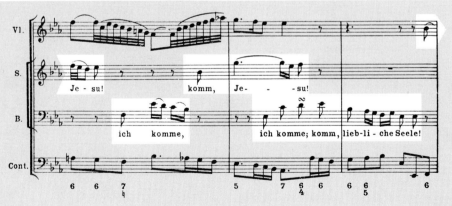

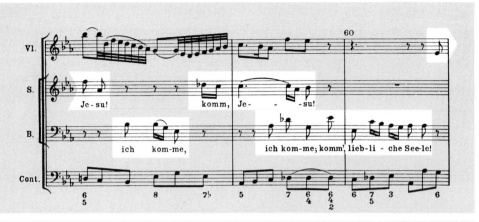

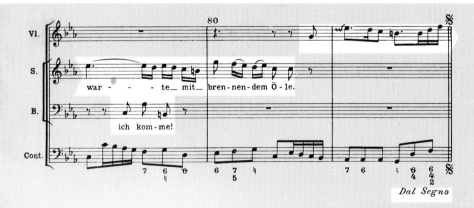

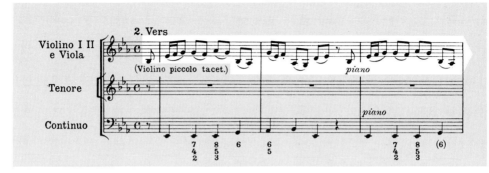

Zi - on hört die Wäch-ter sin - gen,

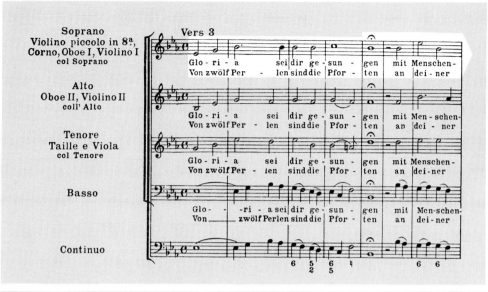

Translation

I

"Awake," the voice of watchmen
calls us from high on the tower,
"Awake, you city of Jerusalem!"

Midnight is this very hour;
they call to us with bright voices:
"Where are you, wise virgins?"

Take cheer, the Bridegroom comes,
arise, take up your lamps!
Hallelujah!
Prepare yourselves for the wedding,
you must go forth to meet him.

II

He comes, he comes, the Bridegroom comes!
Daughters of Zion, come forth,
he is hurrying from on high
into your mother's house.

The Bridegroom comes, who like a roe
and a young hart
leaping upon the hills
brings you the wedding meal.

Wake up, bestir yourselves
to receive the Bridegroom;
there, look, he comes along.

III

Soul: When will you come, my salvation?
Jesus: I am coming, your own.
Soul: I am waiting with burning oil.
 Throw open the hall
 to the heavenly banquet!

Jesus: I open the hall
to the heavenly banquet.
Soul: Come, Jesus!
Jesus: Come, lovely Soul!

I V

Zion hears the watchmen singing,
for joy her very heart is springing,
she wakes and rises hastily.

From heaven comes her friend resplendent,
sturdy in grace, mighty in truth,
her light shines bright, her star ascends.

Now come, you worthy crown,
Lord Jesus, God's own Son,
Hosanna!
We all follow
to the joyful hall
and share the Lord's Supper.

v

Come enter in with me,
my chosen bride!
I have pledged my troth
to you in eternity!
I will set you as a seal upon my heart,
and as a seal upon my arm
and restore delight to your sorrowful eye.
Forget now, o soul,
the anguish, the pain,
which you had to suffer;
on my left you shall rest,
and my right shall kiss you.

V I

Soul: My friend is mine!
Jesus: and I am his!
Both: Love shall separate nothing!

Soul: I will feed with you among heaven's roses,
Jesus: You shall feed with me among heaven's roses,
Both: There fullness of joy, there rapture shall be!

VII

Gloria be sung to you
with men's and angels' tongues,
with harps and beautiful cymbals.

Of twelve pearls are the gates
at your city; we are consorts
of the angels high about your throne.

No eye has ever sensed,
no ear has ever heard
such a delight.
Of this we rejoice,
io, io,
forever *in dulci jubilo*.

TRANSLATED BY
GERHARD HERZ

14. BACH, *Crucifixus* from Mass in B minor (c.1740?)

15. FRANZ JOSEPH HAYDN (1732-1809),
String Quartet in C major, Opus 76, No. 3 (1797)

Ernst Eulenburg Ltd.,
London - Zurich -

II

Poco adagio; cantabile

Var. III

III

Menuett. Allegro

16. WOLFGANG AMADEUS MOZART (1756-1791),
First and third movements from *Eine kleine Nachtmusik* (1787)

I

Ernst Eulenburg Ltd.,
London · Zurich

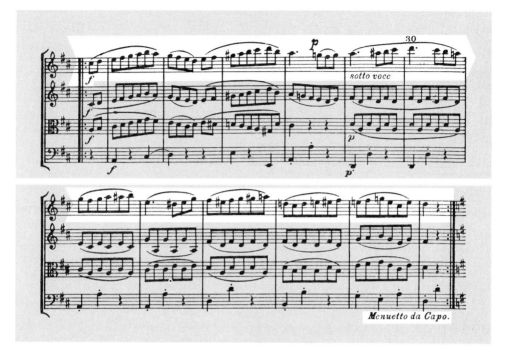

17. MOZART, Three excerpts from *Don Giovanni* (1787)

No. 1, Introduction

Scene — A Garden, Night.

Leporello, in a cloak, discovered watching before the house of Donna Anna; then Donna Anna and Don Giovanni, afterwards the Commandant.

Molto allegro.

Piano.

Strings & Fag.   Strings & Fag.

Vlns.

(wrapt in a dark mantle, impatiently pacing to and fro before the steps
Leporello.   to the palace).

Not-te e gior-no fa - ti - car, per chi nul-la sa gra - dir; pio-va e
On the   go from morn till   night, Run-ning er-rands, nev-er   free, Hard-ly

ven-to sop-por-tar, mangiar ma-le,e mal dor -   mir!
time to snatch a   bite; This is   not the life for   me.

Vo - glio   far il gen-til - uo - mo,   e   non
I   would   like to play the   mas-ter,   Would   no

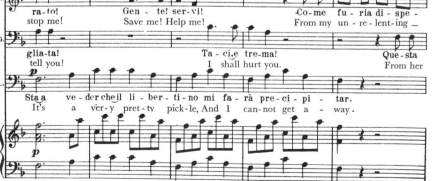

No. 4, Catalogue Aria

in Al - ma-gna due cen-to e trent' u - na,
Down for Eng-land, a hun - dred-e - lev - en;

cen - to in Francia, in Turchia no-vant' u - na; ma, in I -
For San Ma - ri - no a mere nine-ty - sev-en; But prim and

spa - gna, ma in I - spa-gna son già mille e tre! mil-lee tre!
prop-er Spain con - tri-butes a thou-sand-and-three! Can that be?

mil - lee tre! V'han fra que-ste con-ta - di - ne,
Yes, it's three. There are bar-maids, bas-ket-weav-ers,

ca - me-rie - re, cit-ta-di - ne, V'han contesse, ba - ro-nes-se,
There are dair-y-maids and di-vas, Count-less count-ess-es, prin-cess-es,

spagna son già mil-le e tre, mil-le e tre, mil-le e
tri-butes a thou-sand-and-three! You are one ... of those

tre! V'han fra queste conta - di-ne, ca-me - rie - re, ci-ta-di-ne, v'han contesse, ba-ro-
three. Yes, with jealously well-hid . -wives, Weeping wid-ows, mellow mid- And in-nu-mer - a-ble -wives,

nesse, marchesa - ne, prin-ci-pesse, e v'han donne d'o-gni gra-do, d'o-gni for-ma, d'ogni e-
nurses He has suf-fered no re-vers-es; Ev-'ry pos-si - ble con-di-tion, Oc-cu-pa-tion, form and

tà! d'o - gni for - ma, d'o - gni e -
age— All a - rouse his gal - lant

tà! d'o - gni for - ma, d'o-gni e - tà!
rage, All a - rouse his gal - lant rage!

No. 7, Duet: *Là ci darem la mano*

18. MOZART, Symphony in G minor, K. 550 (1788)

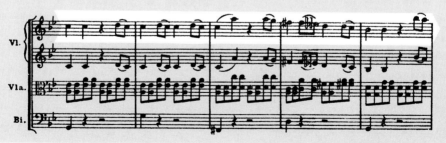

Ernst Eulenburg Ltd., London- Zürich

This edition presents the score of Mozart's second version, with clarinets.

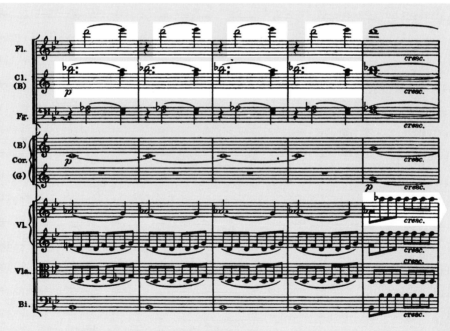

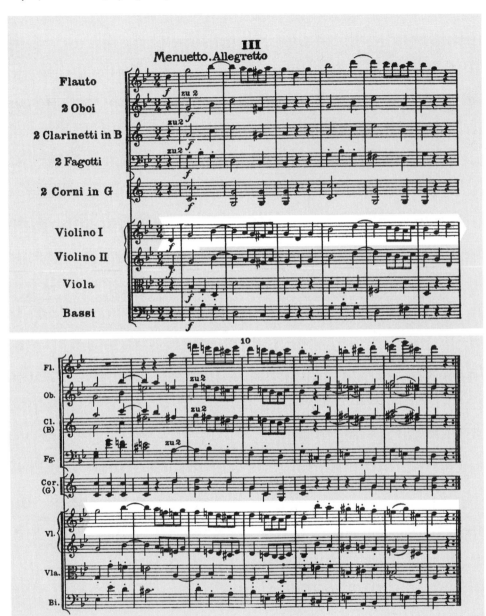

19. LUDWIG VAN BEETHOVEN (1770-1827),
Piano Sonata in C minor, Opus 13 ("Pathetique") (1799)

attacca subito il Allegro.

RONDO.
Allegro.

20. BEETHOVEN, Symphony No. 5 in C minor (1807)

Ernst Eulenburg Ltd.,
London · Zurich ·

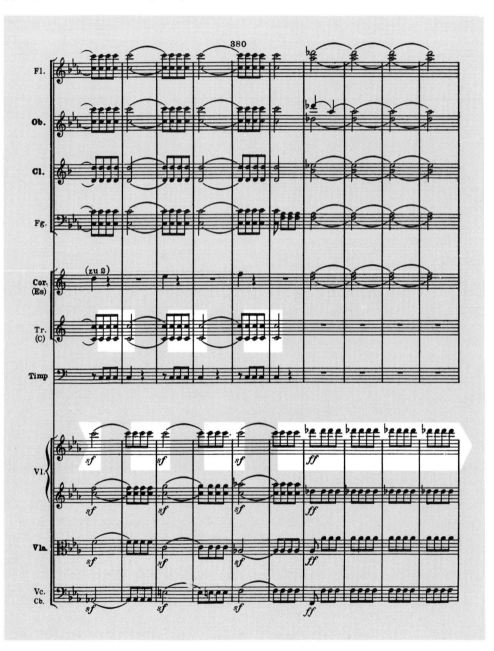

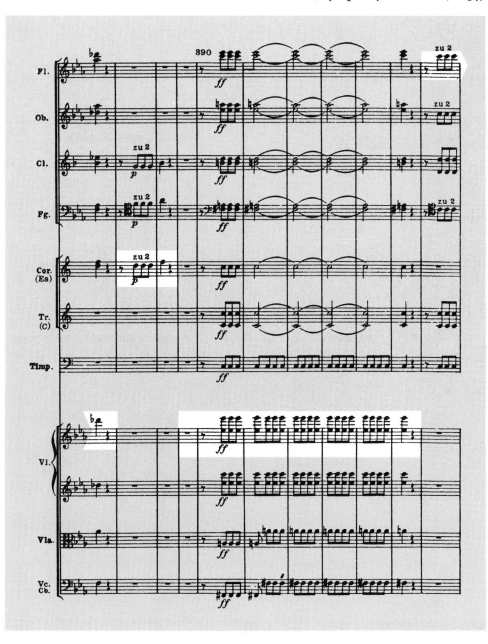

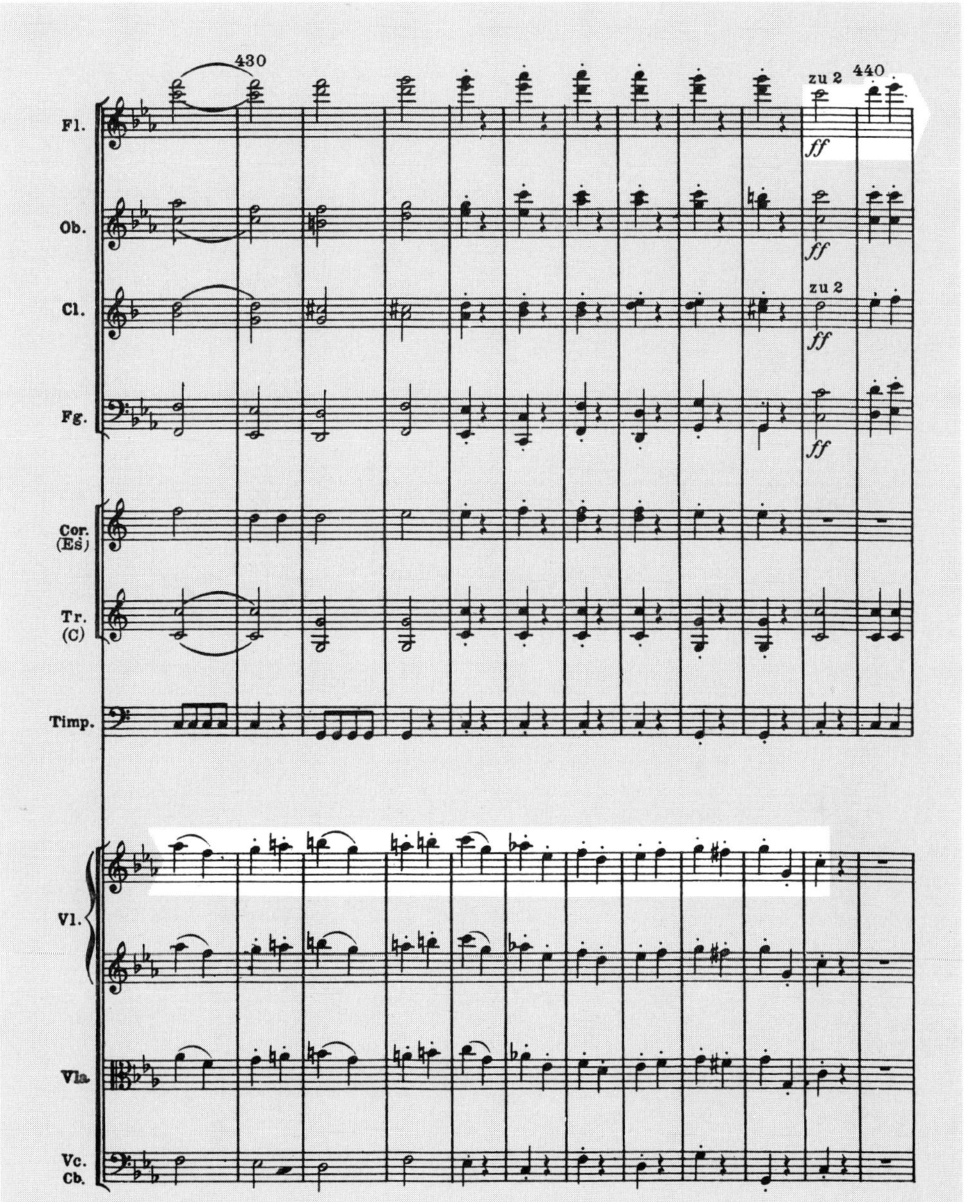
430
440
Fl.
zu 2
ff
Ob.
ff
Cl.
zu 2
ff
Fg.
ff
Cor. (Es)
Tr. (C)
Timp.
Vl.
Vla.
Vc. Cb.

II

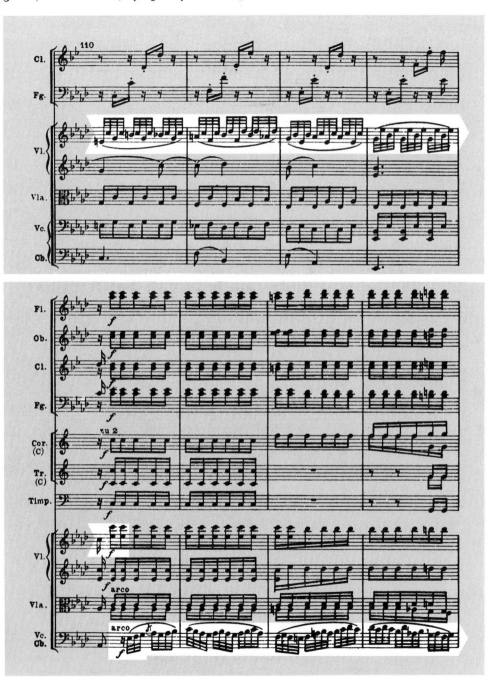

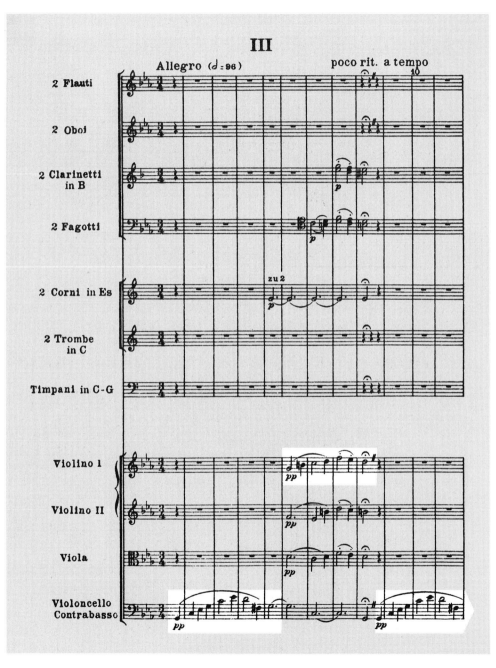

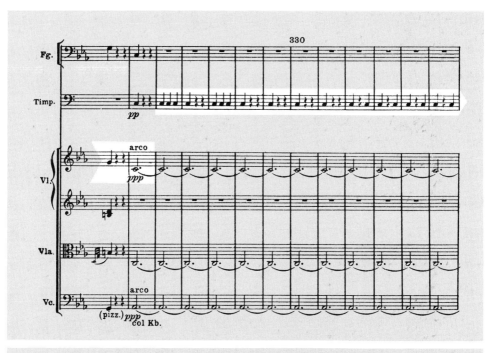

IV

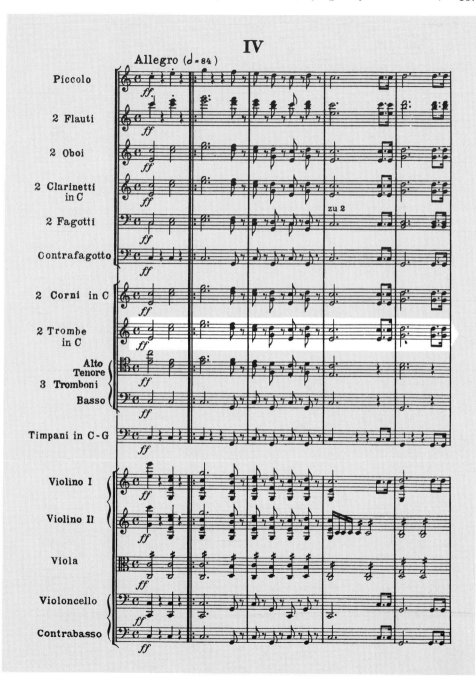

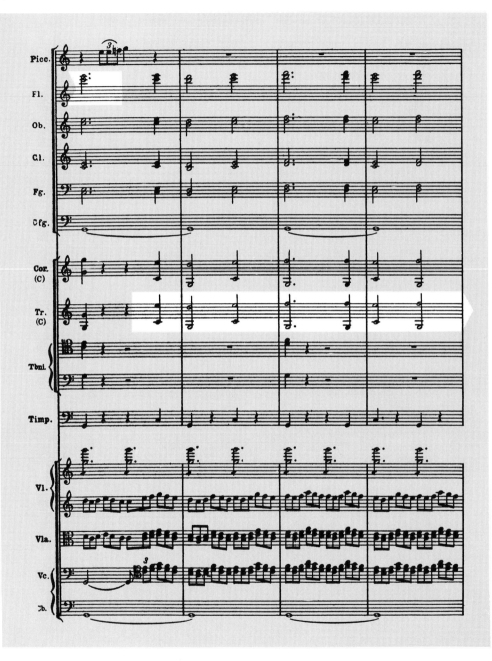

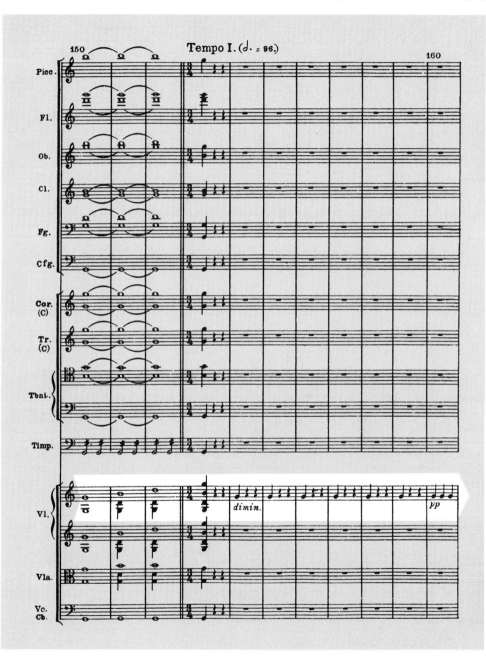

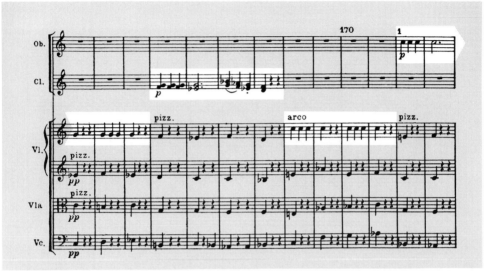

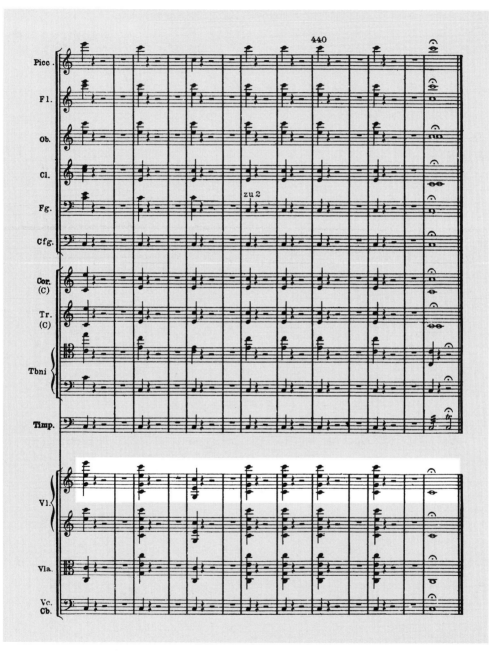

21. FRANZ PETER SCHUBERT (1797-1828), *Heidenröslein* (1815)
(Poem by Goethe)

Sah ein Knab' ein Rös_lein_ stehn, Rös_lein auf der Hei _ den,
Kna_be sprach: ich bre _ che_ dich, Rös_lein auf der Hei _ den,
Und der wil _ de Kna _ be_ brach 'sRös_lein auf der Hei _ den;

war so jung und mor_gen schön, lief er schnell es nah' zu sehn, sah's mit · vie _ len Freu _ den.
Röslein sprach: ich ste _ che dich, dass du e _ wig denkst an mich, und ich will's nicht lei _ den.
Röslein wehr _ te sich und stach, half ihm doch kein Weh und Ach, musst' es e _ ben lei _ den.

Röslein, Röslein, Rös _ lein rot, Röslein auf der Hei _ den.
Röslein, Röslein, Rös _ lein rot, Röslein auf der Hei _ den.
Röslein, Röslein, Rös _ lein rot, Röslein auf der Hei _ den.

Translation

A lad saw a rosebud,
rosebud on the heath;
it was so young in its morning beauty
that he ran to look at it more closely;
he gazed at it with great pleasure.
Rosebud red,
rosebud on the heath.

The lad said: "I'll pick you,
rosebud on the heath!"
The rosebud said: "I'll prick you,
so that you will always think of me,
and I won't stand for it."
Rosebud red,
rosebud on the heath.

And the brutal lad picked
the rosebud on the heath;
the rosebud defended itself and pricked,
yet no grief and lamentation helped it:
it simply had to suffer.
Rosebud red,
rosebud on the heath.

TRANSLATED BY
PHILIP L. MILLER

22. SCHUBERT, *Erlkönig* (1815) (Poem by Goethe)

Translation

Who rides so late through the night and the wind?
It is the father with his child;
he folds the boy close in his arms,
he clasps him securely, he holds him warmly.

"My son, why do you hide your face so anxiously?"
"Father, don't you see the Erlking?
The Erlking with his crown and his train?"
"My son, it is a streak of mist."

"Dear child, come, go with me!
I'll play the prettiest games with you.
Many colored flowers grow along the shore;
my mother has many golden garments."

"My father, my father, and don't you hear
the Erlking whispering promises to me?"
"Be quiet, stay quiet, my child;
the wind is rustling in the dead leaves."

"My handsome boy, will you come with me?
My daughters shall wait upon you;
my daughters lead off in the dance every night,
and cradle and dance and sing you to sleep."

"My father, my father, and don't you see there
the Erlking's daughters in the shadows?"
"My son, my son, I see it clearly;
the old willows look so gray."

"I love you, your beautiful figure delights me!
And if you are not willing, then I shall use force!"
"My father, my father, now he is taking hold of me!
The Erlking has hurt me!"

The father shudders, he rides swiftly on;
he holds in his arms the groaning child,
he reaches the courtyard weary and anxious:
in his arms the child was dead.

TRANSLATED BY
PHILIP L. MILLER

23. SCHUBERT, Fourth movement (Theme and Variations) from Quintet in A major ("Trout") for Violin, Viola, Cello, Double Bass, and Piano (1819?)

Ernst Eulenburg Ltd., London - Zurich

24. HECTOR BERLIOZ (1803-1869), Fifth movement from *Symphonie fantastique* (1830)

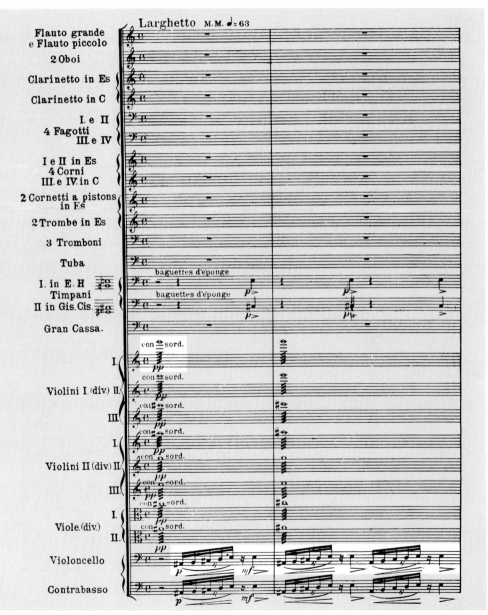

Ernst Eulenburg Ltd., London · Zurich

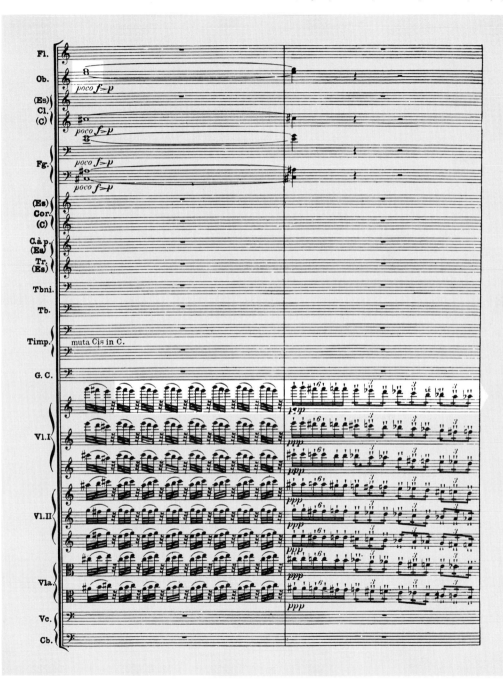

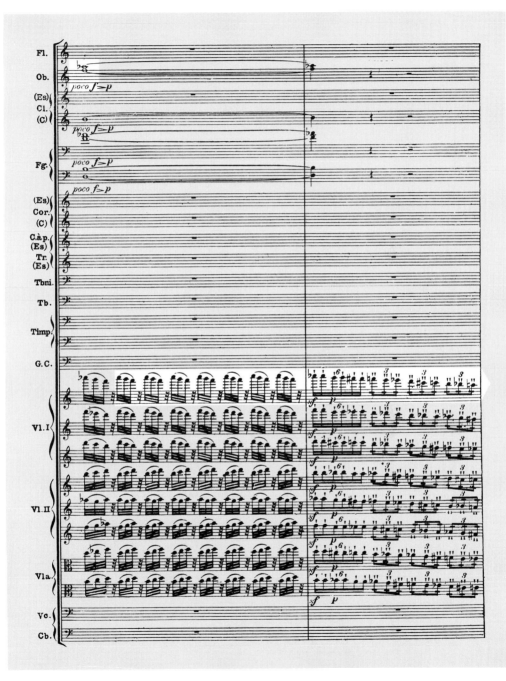

Cmp.
Picc.
Fl.
Ob.
Es)
Cl.
(C)
Fg.
(Es)
Cor.
(C)
C.à p.
(Es)
Tr.
(Es)
Tbni.
(C)
Tb.
(B)
Timp.
G.C.
Vl.
Vla.
Vc.
Cb.
pizz.
pizz.
pizz.

Cmp.
Picc.
Fl.
Ob.
(Es)
Cl.
(C)
Fg.
(Es)
Cor.
(C)
C.à p.
(Es)
Tr.
(Es)
Tbni.
(C)
Tb.
(B)
Timp.
G. C.
Vl.
Vla.
Vc.
Cb.
pizz.
pizz.
pizz.

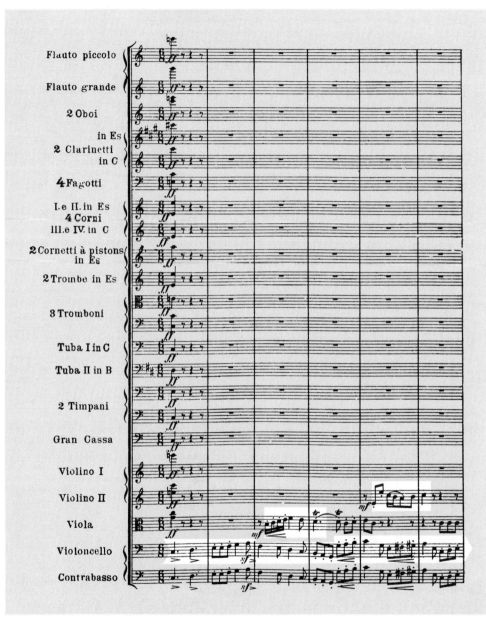

uno sonator de'timpani

(Dies irae et Ronde du Sabbat.)

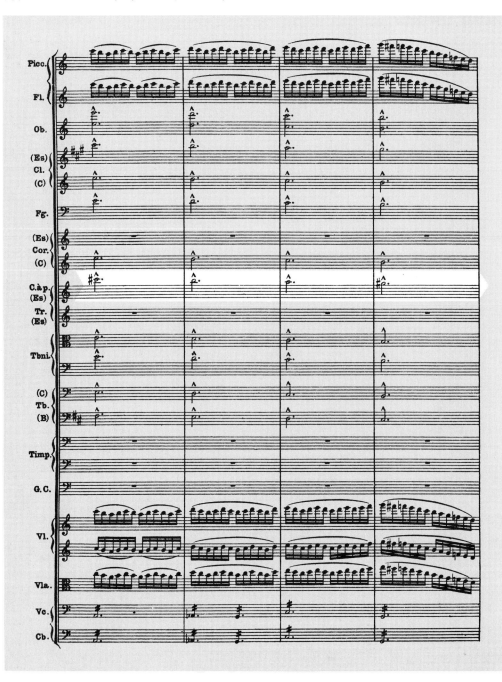

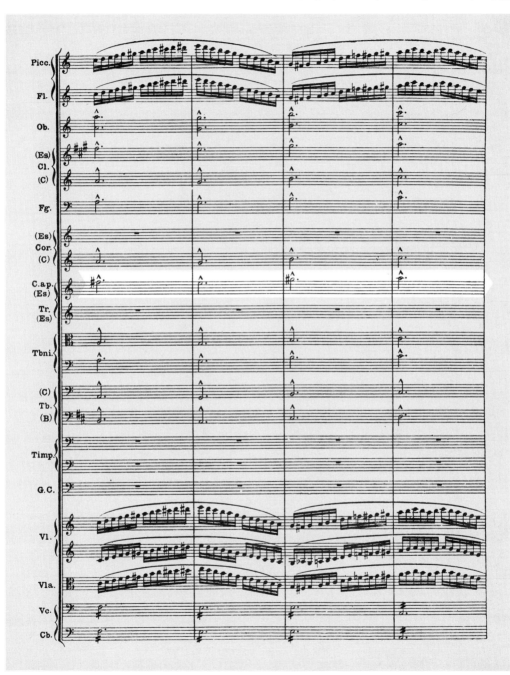

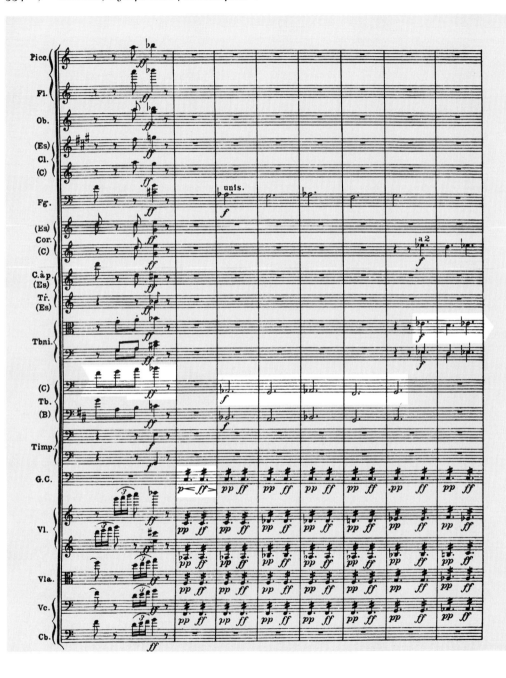

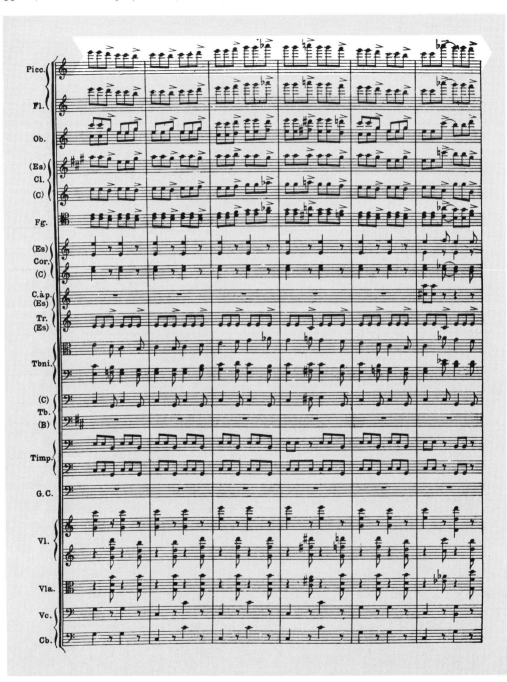

uno Piatto battuto colla bacchetta di spugna.

25. FELIX MENDELSSOHN (1809-1847),
First movement from Violin Concerto in E minor (1844)

Ernst Eulenburg Ltd., London · Zurich ·

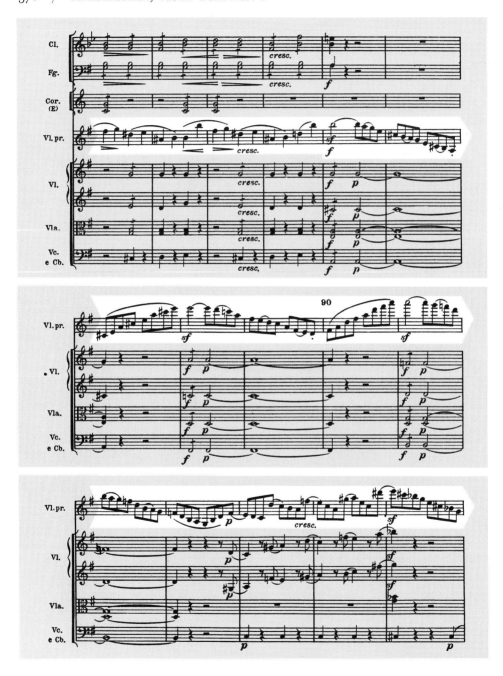

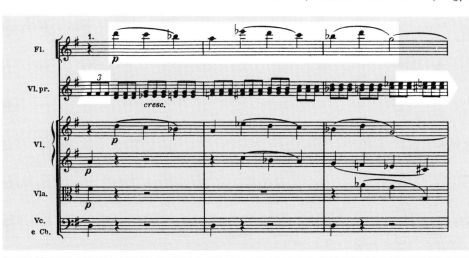

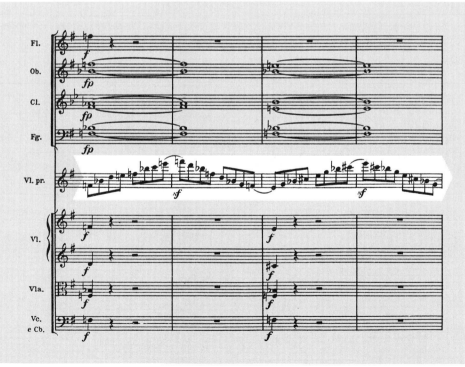

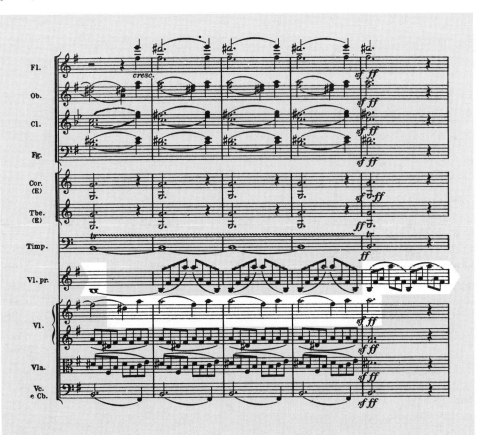

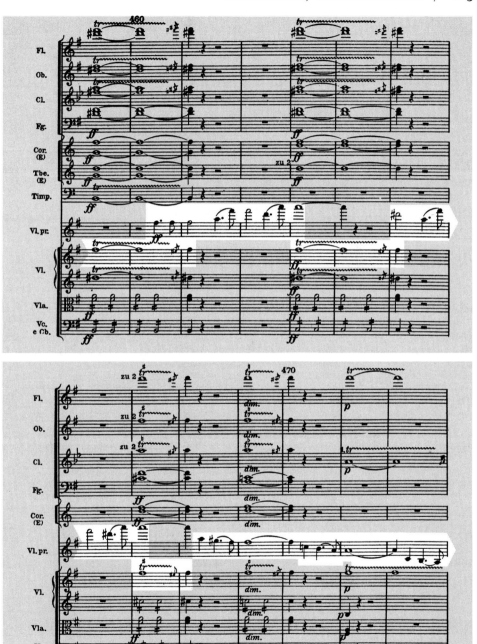

26. FRÉDÉRIC CHOPIN (1810-1849), Mazurka in B-flat major, Opus 7, No. 1 (PUBL. 1832)

27. CHOPIN, Etude in E major, Opus 10, No. 3 (PUBL. 1833)

28. CHOPIN, Prelude in E minor, Opus 28, No. 4 (PUBL. 1839)

29. ROBERT SCHUMANN (1810-1856),
Die beiden Grenadiere (1840) (Poem by Heine)

Translation

To France were returning two grenadiers
who had been captured in Russia;
and when they came to the German land
they hung their heads.

For there they heard the sad news
that France was lost,
the great army defeated and destroyed
and the Emperor a prisoner.

The grenadiers wept together
over the miserable tidings.
One spoke: "Woe is me!
How my old wound burns!"

The other said: "It is all over.
I too would like to die with you,
but I have a wife and child at home
who without me would perish."

"What do I care for wife and child?
I have more important concerns.
Let them go begging if they are hungry—
my Emperor is a prisoner!

"Brother, grant me one request,
if I must die now;
take my body to France with you,
bury me in French earth.

"My cross of honor, with the red ribbon,
you must lay on my heart;
put my rifle in my hand,
and fasten my sword-belt around me.

"So will I lie still and listen,
like a sentry in the grave,
until I hear the noise of cannon
and the hoofs of whinnying horses.

"Then should my Emperor ride over my grave,
with many swords clanking and clashing;
then I shall arise, fully armed, from my grave,
to defend my Emperor!"

TRANSLATED BY
PHILIP L. MILLER

30. RICHARD WAGNER (1813-1883),
Duet from *Die Walküre*, Act I (1856)

(Siegmund allein. Es ist vollständig Nacht geworden; der Saal ist nur noch von einem schwachen Feuer im Herde erhellt.)
(Siegmund alone. It has become quite dark. The hall is only lighted by a dull fire on the hearth.)

Mässig langsam.

(Siegmund lässt sich, nah beim Feuer, auf dem Lager nieder, und brütet in grosser innerer Aufregung eine
(Siegmund sinks on a bench by the fire and broods silently for some time in great agitation.)

Zeitlang schweigend vor sich hin.)

SIEGM.

Ein Schwert verhiess mir der Va - ter, ich fänd' es in höch - ster Noth.__
A sword, my fa - ther fore-told me should serve me in sor - est need.__

Waffen-los fiel ich in Feindes Haus;
Sword-less I come to my foeman's house;

seiner Rache Pfand ra-ste ich hier:__
as a hostage here helpless I lie:__

SIEGM.

ein Weib sah' ich, won - nig und hehr: ent - zü - ckend Ban-gen
a wife saw I, *won-drous and fair* *and bliss-ful tremors*

zehrt mein Herz. Zu der mich nun Sehnsucht zieht, die mit süs - sem Zauber mich
seized my heart. *The wo-man who holds me chained,* *who with sweet en-chant-ment*

sehrt, im Zwan - ge hält sie der Mann, der mich wehr - lo - sen
wounds, *in thrall is held by the man* *who mocks his wea-pon-less*

höhnt. Wäl - se! Wäl - se! Wo ist dein
foe. *Wäl - se! Wäl - se! Where is thy*

SIEGM.

Schwert? Das starke Schwert, das im Sturm ich schwän - ge, bricht mir hervor aus der
sword? The trusty sword, that in fight shall serve me, when from my bo - som out-

Brust, was wü - thend das Herz noch hegt? Was
breaks the fu - ry my heart now bears? What

(Das Feuer bricht zusammen; es fällt aus der aufsprühenden Gluth
plötzlich ein greller Schein auf die Stelle des Eschenstammes;
welche Sieglindes Blick bezeichnet hatte, und an der man jetzt
deutlich einen Schwertgriff haften sieht.)
*(The fire falls together. From the flame which springs up a bright
light strikes on the spot in the ash-stem indicated by Sieglindes
look, on which a sword-hilt is now clearly seen.)*

Tempo I.

Tempo I

gleisst dort hell im Glimmerschein? Welch' ein Strahl bricht aus der Esche Stamm, Des
gleam - eth there from out the gloom? What a beam breaks from the ash-tree's stem! The

Blin - den Au - ge leuch - tet ein Blitz: lu - stig lacht da der Blick. ___
sight-less eye ___ be - hold - eth a flash: gay as laugh-ter its light!___

SIEGM.

schied, traf mich A-bends ihr Schein; selbst der
hence, *fell a gleam on me here;* *e'en the*

al - ten E-sche Stamm er glänz-te in gold'-ner Gluth: da
an cient ash tree's stem shone forth with a gol - den glow. *now*

bleicht die Blü-the, das Licht verlischt; nächtiges Dunkel deckt mir das Au - ge: tief in des Bu-sens
pales the splendour, the light dies out; darkening shadow gathers a-round me: *deep in my breast a-*

(Das Feuer ist gänzlich verloschen: volle Nacht.)
(The fire is quite extinguished: complete darkness.)

(Das Seitengemach öffnet sich leise.)
(The door at the side opens softly.)

Ber - ge glimmt nur noch licht-lo - se Gluth.
lone yet glimmers a dim dy-ing glow.

SIEGL.

Stärk - sten al - lein ward sie be-stimmt.
strong - est a - lone was it de-creed.

O mer-ke wohl, was ich dir
O heed thou well what I now

bestimmt

Langsamer.

mel - de! Der Männer Sip - pe sass hier im Saal, von Hunding zur Hochzeit ge-la - den: er
tell thee! The kinsmen gathered here in the hall, to honour the wedding of Hunding: the

Langsam.

frei - te ein Weib, das un-ge-fragt Schächer ihm schenkten zur Frau. Trau - rig sass ich während sie tranken; ein
wo-man he chose, by him unwooed, mis-creants gave him to wife. Sad I sat the while they were drinking; a

Mässig.

Frem - der trat da her - ein: ein Greis in grau-em Ge-wand; tief
stran - ger en-tered the hall: an old man clad all in grey; low

SIEGL.

stiess er nun in der E - sche Stamm, bis zum Heft haf - tet' es
then he struck in the ash - tree stem; to the hilt bu - ried it

drin:__ dem soll-te der Stahl ge-ziemen, der aus dem Stamm es zög'. Der
lies:__ but one man might win the weapon-he who could draw it forth. Of

Männer Al-le, so kühn sie sich mühten, die Wehr sich Keiner ge-wann; Gä-ste kamen und Gä-ste gingen, die
all the heroes, though bravely they laboured, not one the weapon could win; guests came hither and guests departed, the

Stärk'sten zo-gen am Stahl__keinen Zoll entwich er dem Stamm: dort haf-tet schweigend das
strongest tugged at the steel__ not a whit it stirred in the stem: there cleaves in si - lence the

SIEGL.

Schwert.___ Da wusst' ich wer der war, der mich gram-vol - le ge-
sword.___ *Then knew I who he was who in sor - row greeted*

grüsst: ich weiss auch, wem allein im Stamm das Schwert er be - stimmt.
me: I know too who a-lone shall draw the sword from the stem.

O fänd_____ich ihn
O might_____I to-

heut' und hier, den Freund; käm' er aus Fremden zur ärmsten
day find here the friend; come from a - far to the sad-dest

SIEGM.

stimmt! | Heiss in der Brust brennt mir der Eid, der
creed! | *Hot in my breast burns now the oath that*

mich dir Ed-len vermählt. | Was je ich er-sehnt er-in
weds me e-ver to thee. | *What-e'er I have sought in*

sah' ich in dir; in dir fand ich was je mir gefehlt!
thee now I see; in thee all that has failed me is found!

Lit - test du Schmach, und schmerz-te mich Leid; war ich ge-äch - tet, und
Though thou wert shamed and woe was my lot; though I was scorned and dis-

SIEGL.

Du bist der Lenz nach
Thou art the spring that

dem ich ver - lang - - te in fro - - sti - gen
I have so longed for in frost - - y

Win - - ters Frist. Dich
win - - ter's spell. My

grüss - - te mein Herz mit hei - - li - gem
heart greet - ed thee with bliss - - ful - lest

SIEGL.

zu dir mich nei - gen, dass hell ich schau - e den
to thee still press me, and see more clear - ly the

heh - ren Schein, der dir _____ aus Aug'
ho - ly light that forth from eyes

und Ant - litz bricht, und so süss _____ die Sin - ne mir
and face doth break and so sweet - ly _____ sways _____ all my

zwingt.
sense.

SIEGM.

Im Len - zes - mond leuch - test du
Be - neath spring's moon shi - nest thou

dolce
pp

SIEGL. (ihm wieder in die Augen spähend.)
(again gazing into his eyes.)

Dei-nes Au - - ges Gluth er - glänz - te mir schon: so
Thine eyes' bright glow ere - while on me shone: the

pp
gut gehalten *poco cresc.* *pp*

blick - te der Greis grüs - send auf mich, als der Trau - ri - gen Trost___
stran - ger so glanced, greet - ing the wife, as he soothed with his look___

più p *pp* *poco a poco*

___ er gab. An dem Blick___ er-kannt' ihn sein Kind___ schon wollt' ich beim
her grief. By his glance___ then knew him his child___ al-most by his

accel.
cresc.

Na - - men ihn nennen! Weh-walt heisst du für-
name did I call him! Wehwalt art thou in

Lebhafter.
molto cresc.

einhaltend.
pausing.

Tempo I?
Langsamer.

p

SIEGM.

Tod:_____ No - - thung! No - - thung! so nenn' ich dich Schwert_____
death:_____ No - - thung! No - - thung! so name I thee, sword_____

No - - thung! No - - thung! neid-li-cher Stahl! Zeig' dei-ner Schär-fe schneidenden
No - - thung! No - - thung! conquer-ing steel! Shew now thy bit-ing se - vering

Zahn! her - aus aus der Schei-de zu mir!_____
blade! come forth from thy scab-bard to me!_____

molto cresc.

(Siegmund zieht mit einem gewaltigen Zuck das Schwert aus dem Stamme, und zeigt es der vor Staunen und Entzücken erfassten Sieglinde.)
(With a powerful effort Siegmund pulls the sword from the tree, and shews it to the astonished and enraptured Sieglinde.)

Mässig schnell

f marcato

31. WAGNER, Prelude to *Tristan und Isolde* (1859)

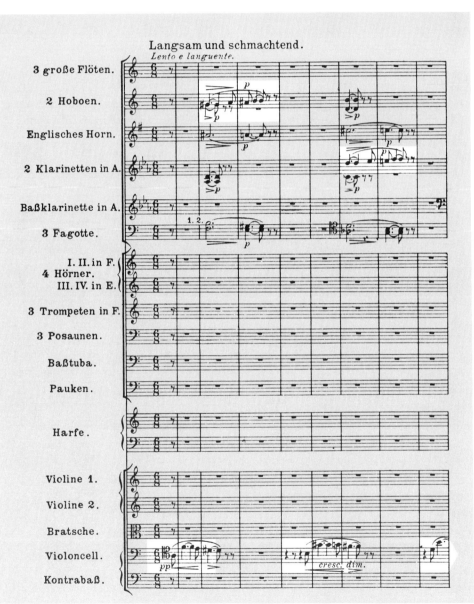

Ernst Eulenburg Ltd.,
London · Zurich

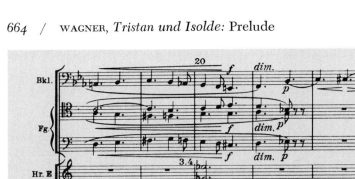

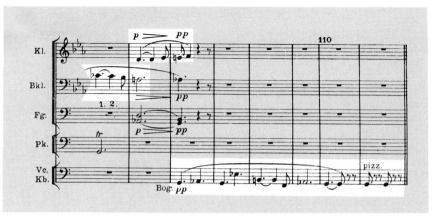

32. GIUSEPPE VERDI (1813-1901),
Scene from *Aïda*, Act III (1871)

Shores of the Nile._ Granite rocks overgrown with palm-trees. On the summit of the rocks, a temple dedicated to Isis, half hidden in foliage. Night; stars and a bright moon.

(From a boat which approaches the shore descend Amneris and Ramphis, followed by some women closely veiled. Guards.)

portando la voce

soc - cor - ri a
Oh, Lend ___ us Thy

to - sa, ma - dre d'im - men - so a - mor, soc - cor - ri a
com - fort, Lead us who stand in awe! Oh, Lend ___ us Thy

to - sa, ma - dre d'im - men - so a - mor, soc - cor - ri a
com - fort, Lead us who stand in awe! Oh, Lend ___ us Thy

Ramphis.

Meno mosso.
(to Amneris)

Vie - ni d'I - si - de al tempio: al - la vi -
Come, let us pray to I - sis! Be - fore her

noi, ___ soc - cor - ri a noi.
com - fort, Oh God - dess on high.

noi, ___ soc - cor - ri a noi.
com - fort, Oh God - dess on high.

noi, ___ soc - cor - ri a noi.
com - fort, Oh God - dess on high.

Meno mosso. ($\bullet$ = 60)

pp *lunga*

con calma

gi - lia del - le tue noz - ze in - vo - ca del - la Di - va il fa - vo - re.
al - tar ask for her bless - ing up - on the ho - ly bond which a - waits you.

I-si-de leg-ge de' mor-ta-li nel co-re;　o-gni mi-ste-ro
Well read is I-sis　in the　heart_ of a mor-tal.　No one can hide a

de-gli u-ma-ni　a le-i　no-to.　Sì;　io pre-ghe-
thought or pas-sion　be-fore the god-dess.　Yes,　and I will

Amneris. *cantabile*

rò　che Ra-da-mès　mi do-ni tut-to il suo cor,　co-me il mio
pray　that Ra-da-mès　may tru-ly give me his heart,_　be-cause my

cor a lui sa-cro è per sem-pre.
own be-longs to him_ for-ev-er.

Ramphis.

An-diamo. Pre-ghe-rai fi-no al-
Come with me! You will pray till the

Aida. (with transport.)

ir._ Un gior-no so — lo di sì dol-ce in-can-to_ u-n' o-ra_u-
sky! Oh, for a day In love to be u — nit-ed, One sin-gle

Amonasro. *cupo.*

n'o — ra di tal_ gio-ia_e poi mo-rir! e poi mo-rir! Pur ram-
hour _ of joy_ sub—-lime And then to die, And then to die! Yet re-

men — ti che a noi l'E — gi-zio im-mi-te, le ca-se, i tem-pii e l'a-re pro-fa-
mem — ber the hang-men he com-mand-ed! No tem-ple, no al-tar, could stay their savage

nò_ tras-se in cep — pi le ver-gi-ni ra-pi-te_ ma-dri_
horde. Shamed, in fet — ters, our wives and daugh-ters brand-ed, Moth-ers,

33. JOHANNES BRAHMS (1833-1897), *Die Mainacht* (PUBL. 1868)
(Poem by Hölty)

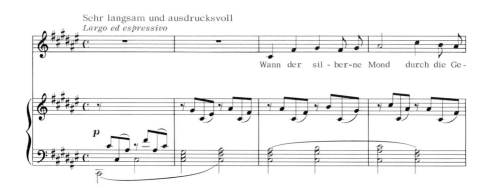

Translation

When the silvery moon gleams through the copse,
and pours his slumbering light over the grass,
and the nightingale warbles,
I wander sadly from bush to bush.

Hidden by the foliage, a pair of doves
coos its delight near by; but I turn away,
seek deeper shadows,
and weep a lonely tear.

When, o smiling image, which like the light of morning
shines through my soul, shall I find you upon the earth?
And the lonely tear
trembles hotter down my cheek!

TRANSLATED BY
PHILIP L. MILLER

34. BRAHMS, Third movement from Symphony No. 3 in F major (1883)

Reprinted with permission of Ernst Eulenburg Ltd., London-Zürich, from the Eulenburg miniature score.

35. MODEST MUSORGSKY (1839-1881),
Field Marshal Death from *Songs and Dances of Death* (1877)

Grokhochet bitva, bleshchut broni,
Orud'ya mednyye revut,
Begut polki, nesutsya koni
I reki krasnyye tekut.

The battle is raging, the armor glitters,
The copper guns thunder out.
The regiments go forth and horses gallop,
And red streams pour forth.

Pylayet polden', lyudi b'yutsya!
Sklonilos' solntze, boĭ sil'neĭ!
Zakat bledneyet, no derutsya
Vragi vsio yarostneĭ i zleĭ!

In the heat of midday, people meander.
And when the sun is setting, the battle expands!
The sunset makes it hard to see,
But the armies fight still more fiercely.

I pala noch' na pole brani.
Druzhiny v mrake razoshlis' . . .
Vsio stikhlo i v nochnom tumane
Stenan' ya k nebu podnyalis'.

And night falls on the field of battle.
The armies separate in the darkness.
All grows quiet, and in the night fog
Moans ascend toward heaven.

Togda ozarena lunoyu,
Na boyevom svoiom kone,
Kosteĭ sverkaya beliznoyu,
Yavilas' smert' i v tishine,

Then, illuminated by moonlight,
Death quietly appears
On his bellicose horse,
Flashing his white bones,

Vnimaya vopli i molitvy
Dovol'stva gordovo polna,
Kak polkovodetz, mesto bitvy
Krugom ob'yekhala ona.

And, listening to wailing and praying,
Is filled with pride and satisfaction
Like a commander riding around the battlefield.
He rides to the top of the hill

Na kholm podnyavshis' oglyanulas',
Ostanovilas', ulybnylas',
I nad ravninoĭ boyevoĭ
Razdalsya golos rokovoĭ:

And looks around and smiles.
And over the battlefield
The voice of fate resounds:
"The battle is over.

"Konchena bitva! Ya vsekh pobedila!
Vse predo mnoĭ vy smirilis' boĭtzy!
Zhizn' vas possorila, ya pomirila,
Druzhno vstavaĭte na smotr,
    mertvetzy!

I have defeated everyone.
You are all humbled before me.
Life made enemies of you. I united you.
Now, dead ones, rise up together for
    examination.

Marshem torzhestvennym mimo proĭdite,
Voĭsko moye ya khochu soschitat'.
V zemlyu potom, svoi kosti slozhite,
Sladko ot zhizni v zemle otdykhat'!

March past solemnly
So I can count my army.
Then place your bones into the ground
To take a rest from life in peace.

Gody nezrimo proĭdut za godami,
V lyudyakh ischeznet i pamyat' o vas.
Ya ne zabudu! I gromko nad vami
Pir budu pravit' v polunochnyĭ chas!

Years will pass by unnoticeably.
People on earth will forget all about you.
But I will not forget! I will celebrate
Your death during the midnight hours.

Plyaskoĭ, tyazholoyu, zemlyu syruyu
Ya pritopchu, chtoby sen' grobovuyu
Kosti pokinut' vo vek ne mogli,
Chtob nikogda vam ne vstat' iz zemli!"

With heavy dance steps, I will stamp
The damp ground so that your bones
Can never leave your graves,
So that you will never rise from the ground."

A. A. GOLENISCHEV-KUTUZOV

TANYA E. MAIRS

36. PETER ILYICH TCHAIKOVSKY (1840-1893),
Romeo and Juliet, Overture-Fantasy (1869)

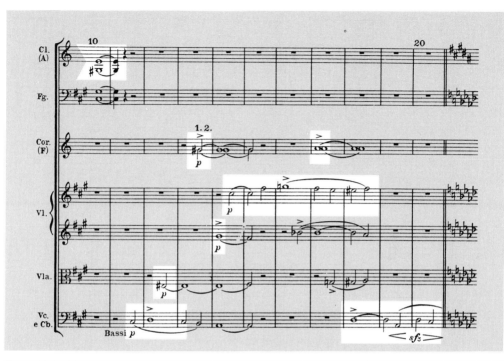

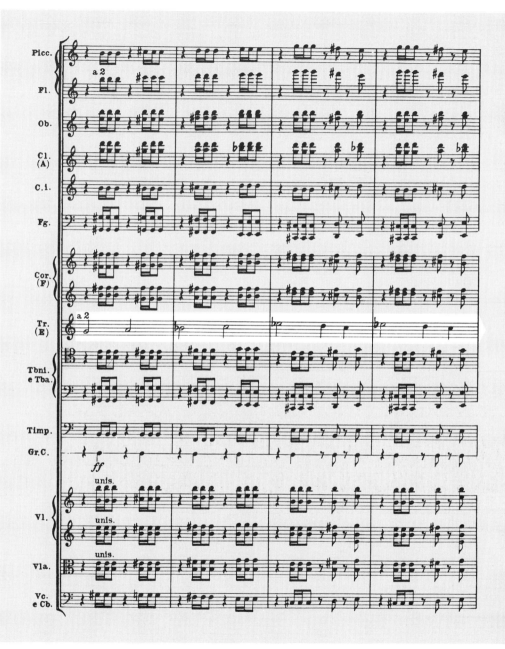

37. TCHAIKOVSKY, Excerpts from *The Nutcracker* (1892)

March

Ernst Eulenburg Ltd. London - Zurich

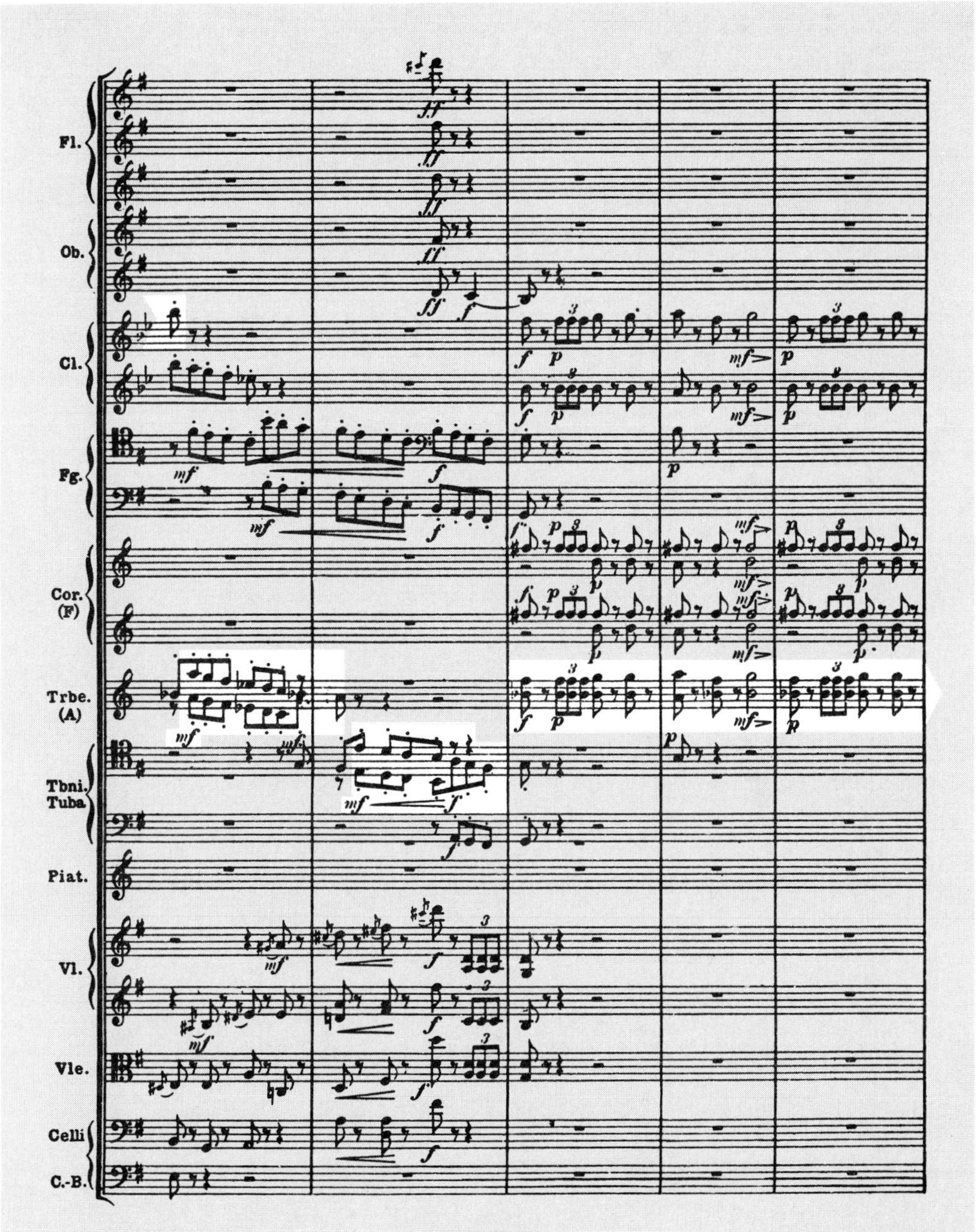
Fl.
Ob.
Cl.
Fg.
Cor. (F)
Trbe. (A)
Tbni. Tuba
Piat.
Vl.
Vle.
Celli
C.-B.

Fl.
Ob.
Cl.
Fg.
Cor. (F)
Trbe. (A)
Tbni.
Tuba
Mit Paukenschlägel.
Piat.
Vl.
Vle.
Celli
C.-B.

Arabian Dance

Dance of the Reed Pipes

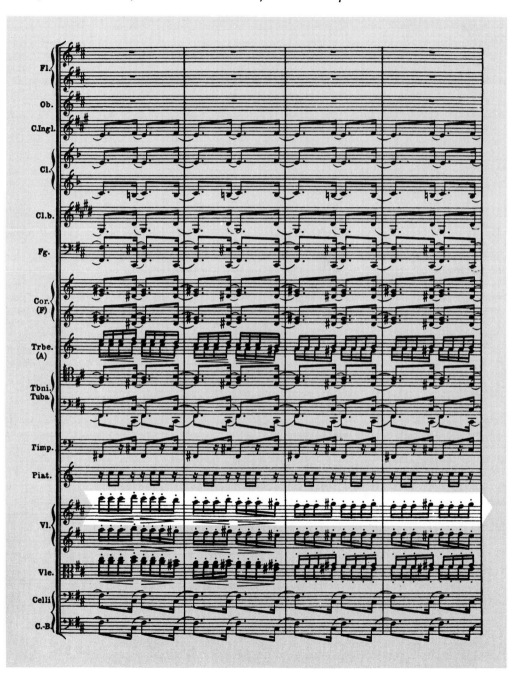

38. GIACOMO PUCCINI (1858-1924),
Scene from *La Bohème*, Act I (1896)

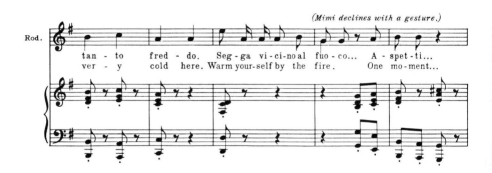

Un poco più mosso ♩ = 126

(reentering, and stopping on the threshold of the door, which remains open)

Mimi: ta - - ta, sven - ta - ta! La chia-ve del - la stan - za
dread - - ful, how dread - ful, I can-not find my door - key,

p con agitazione

Mimi: do - ve l'ho la - scia - ta?
I am so for - get - ful!

Rod.: Non sti - a sul - l'u - -
Don't stay so near the door -

mf

(Mimi's light goes out.)

Mimi: Oh
Good

Rod.: scio; il lu - me va - cil - la al ven - - to.
way; the wind is too strong for your can - - dle.

dolce

(*Searches with her fingers.*)

Mimi: Mi par - ve... / I thought you...

Rod.: in ve - ri - tà! / I thought so too!

rit.

rall. un poco

f

Mimi: Cer - ca? / No - where?

(*Pretends to search, but, guided by Mimi's voice and movements, tries to get near her.*)

Rod.: Cer - co! / No - where!

a tempo

p

f espress.
rall.

(*Mimi stoops to the floor, continuing to search for the key; at this moment Rodolfo reaches her and as he also stoops, his hand encounters hers.*)

p

dim. e rall.

pp
stentate

Andante lento ♩ = 40

Mimi: chia - ma - no Mi - mì, ma il mio no - me è Lu - ci - a.___
al - ways called Mi - mi, but my name is Lu - ci - a.___

Mimi: La sto-ria mia è bre - ve:___ A te-la o a se - ta ri-ca-mo in ca-sa e
My sto-ry is a brief one:___ I earn my liv-ing by sew-ing and em-

Mimi: fuo - ri... Son tran-quil-la e lie - ta ed è mio sva - go far gi - glie
broi-der-ing. Work-ing gives me plea-sure; in lei - sure hours I make lil-ies and

Andante calmo ♩ = 54
dolcemente

Mimi: ro - se.___ Mi piac - cion quel - le co - se che han sì dol - ce ma the
ros - es.___ I' dear - ly love those flow - ers, they de-light and en-

(36)
dolce

molto piano

Allegretto moderato ♩ = 144

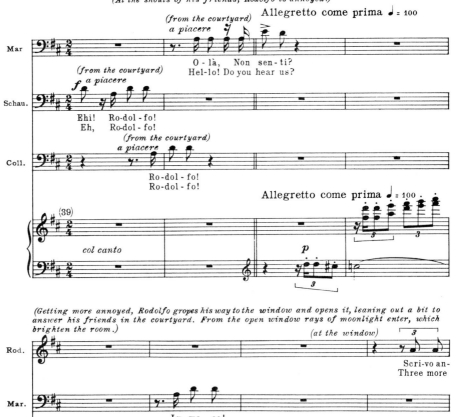

(Mimi goes still nearer the window, The moonlight falls upon her.)

39. HUGO WOLF (1860-1903),
In dem Schatten meiner Locken (1889)

Leicht, zart, nicht schnell.   *sehr zurückhaltend*

In dem Schat - ten mei - ner Lo - cken schlief mir mein Ge - lieb - ter
In the sha - dow of my tress - es, my be - loved to sleep has

a tempo

ein.   Weck' ich ihn nun auf?
gone.   *I'll not wake thee, love,*

Ach nein!   Sorg - - lich
sleep on!   *By the*

In dem Schatten meiner Locken
Schlief mir mein Geliebter ein.
Weck' ich ihn nun auf?—Ach nein!

Sorglich strählt' ich meine krausen
Locken täglich in der Frühe,
Doch umsonst ist meine Mühe,
Weil die Winde sie zersausen,
Lockenschatten, Windessausen
Schläferten den Liebsten ein.
Weck' ich ihn nun auf?—Ach nein!

Hören muss ich, wie ihn gräme,
Dass er schmachtet schon so lange,
Dass ihm Leben geb' und nehme
Diese meine braune Wange.
Und er nennt mich seine Schlange,
Und doch schlief er bei mir ein.
Weck' ich ihn nun auf?—Ach nein!

FROM THE *Spanish Songbook* OF
PAUL HEYSE AND EMANUEL GEIBEL

In the shadow of my curls
my lover lies asleep.
Shall I wake him? Ah, no!

Carefully I have combed my curly
locks every morning,
but my trouble is in vain,
because the winds dishevel them.
Shadow of curls, rush of wind,
put my lover to sleep.
Shall I wake him? Ah, no!

I must listen to his complaining
that he languished so long,
that his whole life depends
on these brown cheeks of mine.
And he calls me his serpent,
and yet he sleeps beside me.
Shall I wake him? Ah, no!

PHILIP L. MILLER

40. CLAUDE DEBUSSY (1862-1918),
Prelude to "The Afternoon of a Faun" (1894)

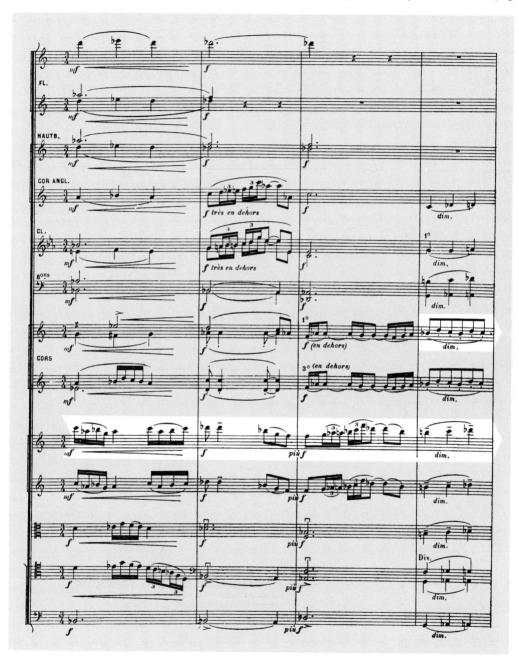

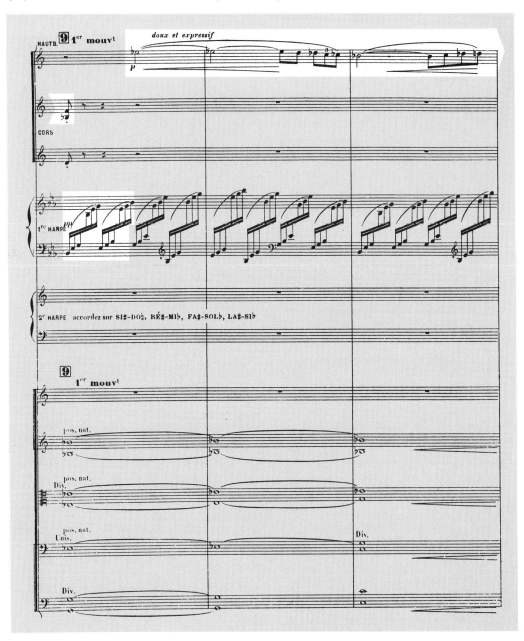

41. ARNOLD SCHOENBERG (1874-1951),
Vergangenes from Five Pieces for Orchestra, Opus 16 (1949)

42. CHARLES IVES (1874-1954),
General William Booth Enters Into Heaven (1914)
(Poem by Vachel Lindsay)

*Both small and large notes in voice part are sung if there is a chorus.

Walk - ing lep - ers fol - lowed rank on rank, Lurch-ing brav - oes from the ditch - es dank

Drabs from the al - ley - ways and drug fiends

pale.___ Minds still pas-sion rid - den, soul powers frail:___ Ver - min - eat - en saints with___ moul - dy

breath, Un - washed___ legions with the ways of ___ Death (Are ___ you ___ washed ___ in the blood of the

Lamb? Are you washed in the blood of the Lamb?)___

43. BÉLA BARTÓK (1881-1945), First movement from Concerto for Orchestra (1943)

Duration of 1st movement approx. 9'48"

44. IGOR STRAVINSKY (1882-1971),
Opening scene from *Petrushka* (1911)

This edition presents the score of Stravinsky's original 1911 version.

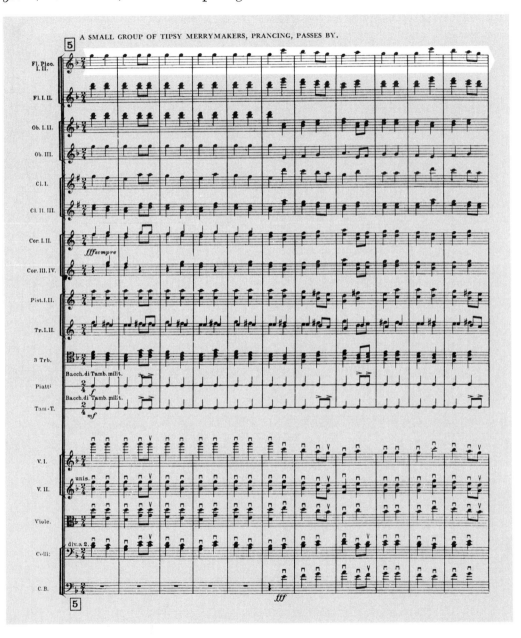

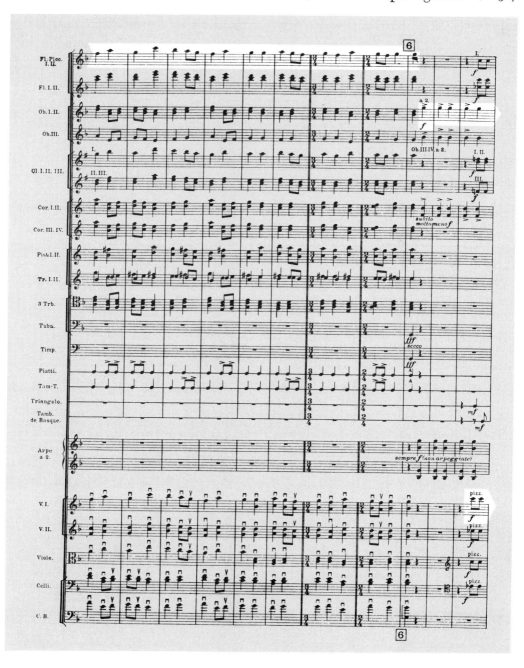

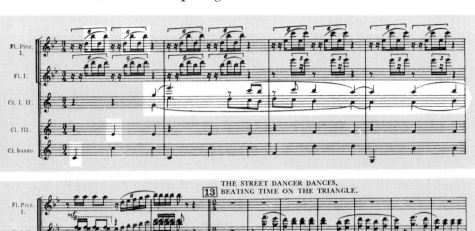

THE STREET DANCER DANCES,
BEATING TIME ON THE TRIANGLE.

*THE ORGAN-GRINDER, CONTINUING TO TURN THE CRANK WITH ONE HAND, PLAYS
THE CORNET WITH THE OTHER.

*THE ORGAN-GRINDER RESUMES PLAYING THE CORNET.

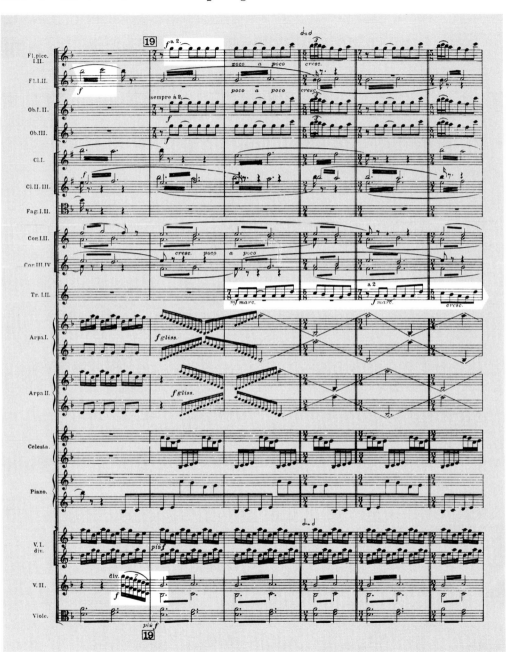

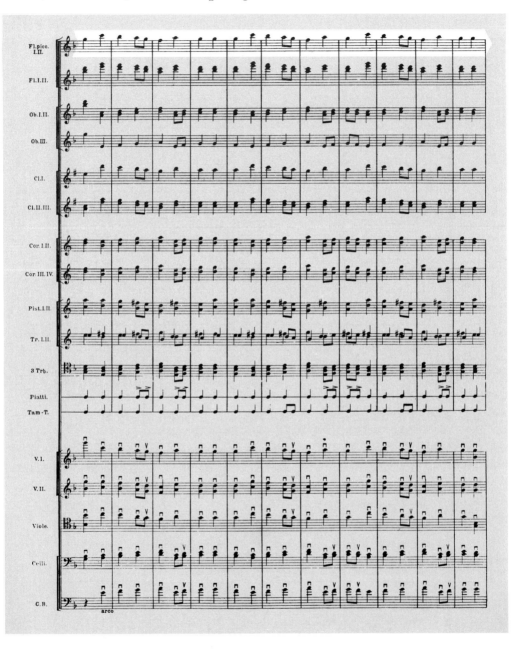

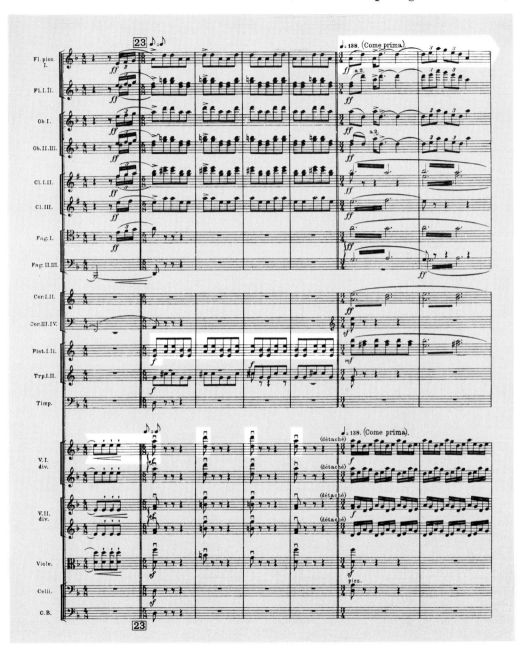

24
Fl. picc. I.
Fl. I. II.
a 2.
Ob. I.
Ob. II. III.
Cl. I. II.
Cl. III.
Fag. I.
Fag. II. III.
Cor. I. II.
II.
Cor III. IV.
Pist I. II.
I.
Tr. I. II.
Tr. III e Tuba
Timp.
V. I. div.
simile
V. II. div.
non div.
simile
Viole
simile
arco
Celli
simile
C. B.
24

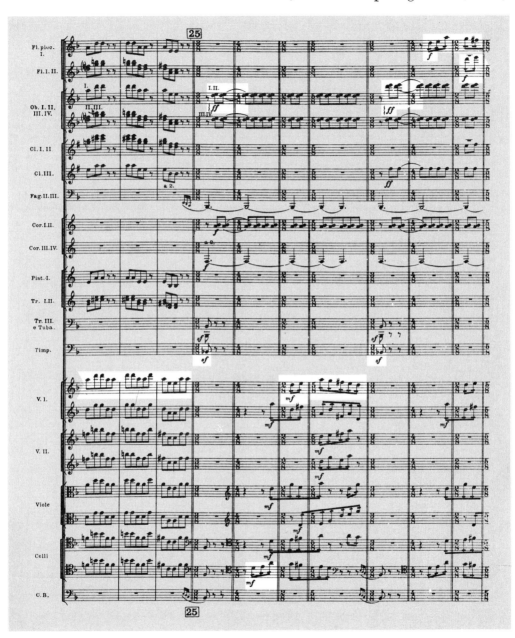

26
Fl. picc. I.
Fl. I. II.
Ob. I. II. III. IV.
Cl. I. II. III.
Fag. I. II. III.
Cor. I. II.
Cor. III. IV.
Pist. I. II.
Tr. I. II.
Tr. III. e Tuba
Timp.
V. I.
V. II.
Viole
Celli
C. B.
sff sempre
unis
non div.
più f
26

45. STRAVINSKY, *Soldier's March* from *L'Histoire du soldat* (1918)

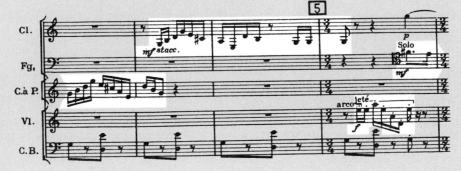

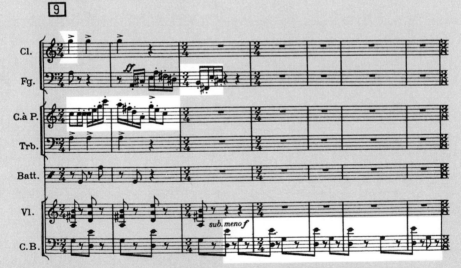

*) Tenir dans la main droite une baguette en jonc à tête en capoc et se servir de celle-ci pour frapper le tambour de basque et la caisse claire; dans la main gauche - la mailloche pour frapper la grosse caisse

*)Pour les baguettes et leur distribution comme ci-dessus

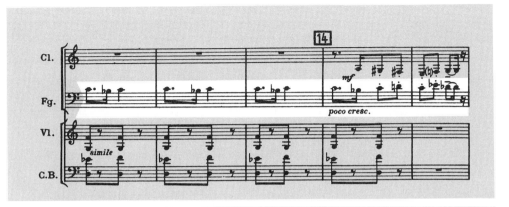

46. STRAVINSKY, First movement from *Symphony of Psalms* (1930)

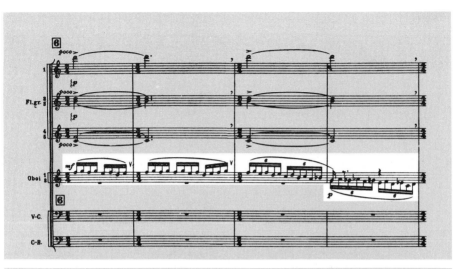

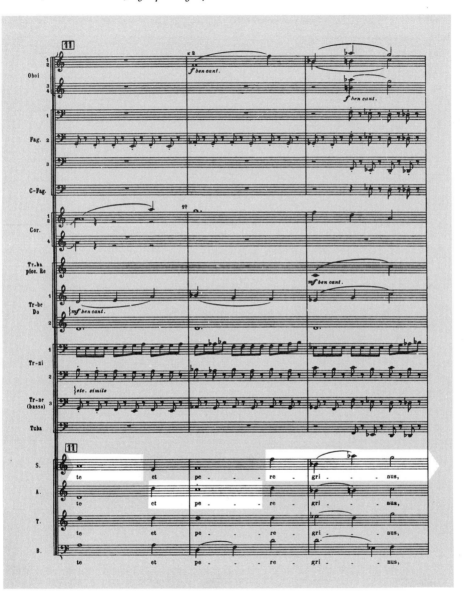

Translation

Hear my prayer, O Lord, and give ear unto my cry;
hold not Thy peace at my tears; for I am a stranger
with Thee, and sojourner, as all my fathers were. O
spare me, that I may recover strength: before I go
hence, and be no more.

PSALM 39 (KING JAMES VERSION),
VERSES 12-13

47. ANTON WEBERN (1883-1945),
Pieces for Orchestra, Opus 10, Nos. 3 and 4 (1913)

III.

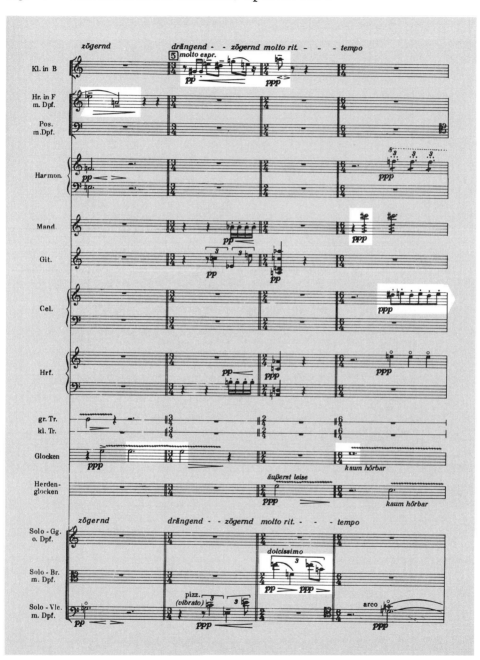

IV.

48. AARON COPLAND (b. 1900),
Opening scene from *Billy the Kid* (1938)

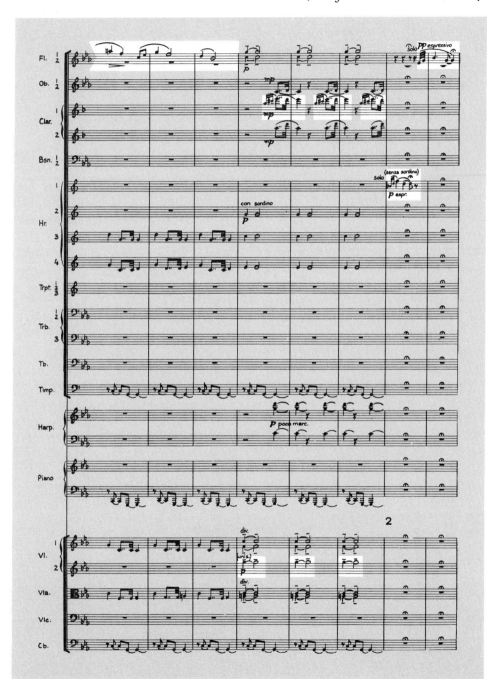

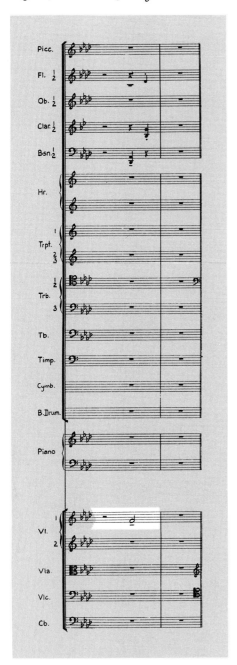

Appendix A

Reading an Orchestral Score

CLEFS

The music for some instruments is written in clefs other than the familiar treble and bass. In the following example, middle C is shown in the four clefs used in orchestral scores:

The *alto clef* is primarily used in viola parts. The *tenor clef* is employed for cello, bassoon, and trombone parts when these instruments play in a high register.

TRANSPOSING INSTRUMENTS

The music for some instruments is customarily written at a pitch different from their actual sound. The following list, with examples, shows the main transposing instruments and the degree of transposition.

Instrument	*Transposition*	*Written Note*	*Actual Sound*
Piccolo, Celesta	sound an octave higher than written		
Trumpet in F	sound a fourth higher than written		
Trumpet in E	sound a major third higher than written		

Instrument	Transposition	Written Note	Actual Sound
Clarinet in E♭, Trumpet in E♭	sound a minor third higher than written		
Trumpet in D	sound a major second higher than written		
Clarinet in B♭, Trumpet in B♭, Cornet in B♭, Horn in B♭ alto	sound a major second lower than written		
Clarinet in A Trumpet in A Cornet in A	sound a minor third lower than written		
Horn in G	sound a fourth lower than written		
English horn, Horn in F	sound a fifth lower than written		
Horn in E	sound a minor sixth lower than written		
Horn in E♭	sound a major sixth lower than written		
Contrabassoon, Horn in C Double bass	sound an octave lower than written		
Bass clarinet in B♭ (written in treble clef)	sound a major ninth lower than written		
(written in bass clef)	sound a major second lower than written		
Bass clarinet in A (written in treble clef)	sound a minor tenth lower than written		
(written in bass clef)	sound a minor third lower than written		

Appendix B

Instrumental Names and Abbreviations

The following tables set forth the English, Italian, German, and French names used for the various musical instruments in these scores, and their respective abbreviations. A table of the foreign-language names for scale degrees and modes is also provided.

WOODWINDS

English	Italian	German	French
Piccolo (Picc.)	Flauto piccolo (Fl. Picc.)	Kleine Flöte (Kl. Fl.)	Petite flûte
Flute (Fl.)	Flauto (Fl.); Flauto grande (Fl. gr.)	Grosse Flöte (Fl. gr.)	Flûte (Fl.)
Alto flute	Flauto contralto (fl.c-alto)	Altflöte	Flûte en sol
Oboe (Ob.)	Oboe (Ob.)	Hoboe (Hb.); Oboe (Ob.)	Hautbois (Hb.)
English horn (E. H.)	Corno inglese (C. or Cor. ingl., C.i.)	Englisches Horn (E. H.)	Cor anglais (C. A.)
Sopranino clarinet	Clarinetto piccolo (clar. picc.)		
Clarinet (C., Cl., Clt., Clar.)	Clarinetto (Cl. Clar.)	Klarinette (Kl.)	Clarinette (Cl.)
Bass clarinet (B. Cl.)	Clarinetto basso (Cl. b., Cl. basso, Clar. basso)	Bass Klarinette (Bkl.)	Clarinette basse (Cl. bs.)
Bassoon (Bsn., Bssn.)	Fagotto (Fag., Fg.)	Fagott (Fag., Fg.)	Basson (Bssn.)
Contrabassoon (C. Bsn.)	Contrafagotto (Cfg., C. Fag., Cont. F.)	Kontrafagott (Kfg.)	Contrebasson (C. bssn.)

BRASS

English	*Italian*	*German*	*French*
French horn (Hr., Hn.)	Corno (Cor., C.)	Horn (Hr.) [*pl.* Hörner (Hrn.)]	Cor; Cor à pistons
Trumpet (Tpt., Trpt., Trp., Tr.)	Tromba (Tr.)	Trompete (Tr., Trp.)	Trompette (Tr.)
Trumpet in D	Tromba piccola (Tr. picc.)		
Cornet	Cornetta	Kornett	Cornet à pistons (C. à p., Pist.)
Trombone (Tr., Tbe., Trb., Trm., Trbe.)	Trombone [*pl.* Tromboni (Tbni., Trni.)]	Posaune (Ps., Pos.)	Trombone (Tr.)
Tuba (Tb.)	Tuba (Tb, Tba.)	Tuba (Tb.) [*also* Basstuba (Btb.)]	Tuba (Tb.)

PERCUSSION

English	*Italian*	*German*	*French*
Percussion (Perc.)	Percussione	Schlagzeug	Batterie (Batt.)
Kettledrums (K. D.)	Timpani (Timp., Tp.)	Pauken (Pk.)	Timbales
Snare drum (S. D.)	Tamburo piccolo (Tamb. picc.) Tamburo militare (Tamb. milit.)	Kleine Trommel Kl. Tr.)	Caisse claire (C. cl.) Tambour militaire (Tamb. milit.)
Bass drum (B. drum)	Gran cassa (Gr. Cassa, Gr. C., G. C.)	Grosse Trommel (Gr. Tr.)	Grosse caisse (Gr. c.)
Cymbals (Cym., Cymb.)	Piatti (P., Ptti., Piat.)	Becken	Cymbales
Tam-Tam (Tam-T.)			
Tambourine (Tamb.)	Tamburino (Tamb.)	Schellentrommel	Tambour de Basque (T. de B., Tamb. de Basque)

English	Italian	German	French
Triangle (Trgl., Tri.)	Triangolo (Trgl.)	Triangel	Triangle (Triang.)
Glockenspiel (Glocken.)	Campanelli (Cmp.)	Glockenspiel	Carillon
Bells (Chimes)	Campane (Cmp.)	Glocken	Cloches
Antique Cymbals	Crotali	Antiken Zimbeln	Cymbales antiques
Sleigh Bells	Sonagli (Son.)	Schellen	Grelots
Xylophone (Xyl.)	Xilofono	Xylophon	Xylophone
Cowbells		Herdenglocken	

STRINGS

English	Italian	German	French
Violin (V., Vl., Vln, Vi.)	Violino (V., Vl., Vln.)	Violine (V., Vl., Vln.)	Violon (V., Vl., Vln.)
		Geige (Gg.)	
Viola (Va., Vl., *pl.* Vas.)	Viola (Va., Vla.) *pl.* Viole (Vle.)	Bratsche (Br.)	Alto (A.)
Violoncello, Cello (Vcl., Vc.)	Violoncello (Vc., Vlc., Vcllo.)	Violoncell (Vc., Vlc.)	Violoncelle (Vc.)
Double bass (D. Bs.)	Contrabasso (Cb., C. B.) *pl.* Contrabassi or Bassi (C. Bassi, Bi.)	Kontrabass (Kb.)	Contrebasse (C. B.)

OTHER INSTRUMENTS

English	Italian	German	French
Harp (Hp., Hrp.)	Arpa (A., Arp.)	Harfe (Hrf.)	Harpe (Hp.)
Piano	Pianoforte (P.-f., Pft.)	Klavier	Piano
Celesta (Cel.)			
Harpsichord	Cembalo	Cembalo	Clavecin
Harmonium (Harmon.)			
Organ (Org.)	Organo		
Guitar		Gitarre (Git.)	
Mandoline (Mand.)			

Note on Baroque Instruments

In the Baroque works, certain older instruments, not used in the modern orchestra, were required by the composers; the following list defines these terms.

Continuo. A method of indicating an accompanying part by the bass notes only, together with figures designating the chords to be played above them. In general practice, the chords are played on a harpsichord or organ, while a viola da gamba or cello doubles the bass notes.

Con un organo di legno e un chitarone. With a small portative organ and a bass lute (as continuo instruments).

Corno. Although this term usually designates the French horn, in the Bach Cantata No. 140 it refers to the *cornett,* or *zink*—a wooden trumpet without valves.

Taille (Tail.). In the Bach Cantata No. 140, this term indicates a tenor oboe or English horn.

Violino piccolo. A small violin, tuned a fourth higher than the standard violin.

Violone (V.). A string instrument intermediate in size between the cello and the double bass. (In modern performances, the double bass is commonly substituted.)

Names of Scale Degrees and Modes

SCALE DEGREES

English	Italian	German	French
C	do	C	ut
C-sharp	do diesis	Cis	ut dièse
D-flat	re bemolle	Des	ré bémol
D	re	D	ré
D-sharp	re diesis	Dis	ré dièse
E-flat	mi bemolle	Es	mi bémol
E	mi	E	mi
E-sharp	mi diesis	Eis	mi dièse
F-flat	fa bemolle	Fes	fa bémol
F	fa	F	fa
F-sharp	fa diesis	Fis	fa dièse
G-flat	sol bemolle	Ges	sol bémol
G	sol	G	sol
G-sharp	sol diesis	Gis	sol dièse
A-flat	la bemolle	As	la bémol
A	la	A	la
A-sharp	la diesis	Ais	la dièse
B-flat	si bemolle	B	si bémol
B	si	H	si
B-sharp	si diesis	His	si dièse
C-flat	do bemolle	Ces	ut bémol

MODES

major	maggiore	dur	majeur
minor	minore	moll	mineur

Appendix C

Glossary of Musical Terms Used in the Scores

The following glossary is not intended to be a complete dictionary of musical terms, nor is knowledge of all these terms necessary to follow the scores in this book. However, as the listener gains experience in following scores, he will find it useful and interesting to understand the composer's directions with regard to tempo, dynamics, and methods of performance.

In most cases, compound terms have been broken down in the glossary and defined separately, as they often recur in varying combinations. A few common foreign-language particles are included in addition to the musical terms. Note that names and abbreviations for instruments and for scale degrees will be found in Appendix B.

a. The phrases *a 2, a 3* (etc.) indicate that the part is to be played in unison by 2, 3 (etc.) players; when a simple number (1., 2., etc.) is placed over a part, it indicates that only the first (second, etc.) player in that group should play.

accompagnato (accomp.). In a continuo part, this indicates that the chord-playing instrument resumes (cf. *tasto solo*).

accordez. Tune the instrument as specified.

accelerando. Growing faster.

adagio. Slow, leisurely.

ad libitum (ad lib.). An indication giving the performer liberty to: (1) vary from strict tempo; (2) include or omit the part of some voice or instrument; (3) include a cadenza of his own invention.

affettuoso. With emotion.

affrettando (affrett.). Hastening a little.

agitato. Agitated, excited.

agitazione. Agitation.

alla. In the style of

allargando (allarg.). Growing broader.

allegretto. A moderately fast tempo (between allegro and andante).

allegro. A rapid tempo (between allegretto and presto).

allmählich. Gradually.

alto, altus (A.). The deeper of the two main divisions of women's (or boys') voices.

amoroso. Lovingly, amorously.

andante. A moderately slow tempo (between adagio and allegretto).

andantino. A moderately slow tempo.

an dem Griffbrett (a.d.G.). Played on the fingerboard.

anima. Spirit, animation.

animando. With increasing animation.

animato, animé. Animated.

a piacere. The execution of the passage is left to the performer's discretion.

appassionato. Impassioned.

arco. Played with the bow.

armonioso. Harmoniously.

arpeggiando (arpeg.). Played in harp style, i.e. the notes of the chord played in quick succession rather than simultaneously.

assai. Very.

a tempo. At the (basic) tempo.

attacca. Begin what follows without pausing.

auf dem. On the (as in *auf dem G*, on the G string).

äusserst. Extremely.

bacchetto di tamburo militare (bacch. di tamb. milit.). Snare-drum sticks.

baguettes d'éponge. Sponge-headed drumsticks.

bass, basso, bassus (B.). The lowest male voice.

belebend. With increasing animation.

belebt. Animated.

ben. Very.

bestimmt. Energetic.

bewegt. Agitated.

bewegter. More agitated.

bien. Very.

Bogen (Bog.). Played with the bow.

bouché. Muted.

bravura. Boldness.

breit. Broadly.

brio. Spirit, vivacity.

cadenza. An extended passage for solo instrument in free, improvisatory style.

calma, calmo. Calm, calmly.

cantabile (cant.). In a singing style.

canto. Voice (as in *col canto*, a direction for the accompaniment to follow the solo part in tempo and expression).

cantus. An older designation for the highest part in a vocal work.

changez. Change (usually an instruction to re-tune a string or an instrument).

circa (ca.). About, approximately.

col, coll'. With the.

come prima. As at first; as previously.

con. With.

continuierlich. Continually.

corda. String; for example, *seconda (2a) corda* is the second string (the A string on the violin).

coro. Chorus.

coulisse. Wings (of a theater).

court. Short, staccato.

crescendo (cresc.). An increase in volume.

cuivré. Played with a harsh, blaring tone.

cupo. Dark, veiled.

da capo (D.C.). Repeat from the beginning.

dal segno. Repeat from the sign.

Dämpfer (Dpf.). Damper.

dans. In.

début. Beginning.

decrescendo (decresc., decr.). A decreasing of volume.

détaché. With a broad, vigorous bow stroke, each note bowed singly.

diminuendo (dim., dimin.). A decreasing of volume.

distinto. Distinct, clear.

divisés, divisi (div.). Divided; indicates that the instrumental group should be divided into two parts to play the passage in question.

dolce. Sweetly and softly.

dolcemente. Sweetly.

dolcissimo (dolciss.). Very sweetly.

doux. Sweetly.

drängend. Pressing on.

e. And.

einige. A few.

en animant. Becoming more animated.

enchainez. Continue to the next material without pause.

en dehors. With emphasis.

espansione. Expansion, broadening.

espressione intensa. Intense expression.

espressivo (espress., espr.). Expressively.

et. And.

etwas. Somewhat, rather.

expressif. Expressively.

fiero. Fiercely.

fine. End, close.

fliessend. Flowing.

flutter-tongue. A special tonguing technique for wind instruments, producing a rapid trill-like sound.

forte (f). Loud.

fortissimo (ff). Very loud (*fff* indicates a still louder dynamic).

forza. Force.

fuga. Fugue.

fuoco. Fire, spirit.

gebunden. Legato.

geteilt (get.). Divided; indicates that the instrumental group should be divided into two parts to play the passage in question.

giusto. Moderately.

gli altri. The others.

glissando (gliss.). Rapid scales produced by running the fingers over all the strings.

gradamente. Gradually.

grande. Large, great.

grande taille. Large size.

grave. Slow, solemn.

guerra. War (*alla guerra,* in warlike fashion).

gut gehalten. Well sustained.

H . In the Schoenberg work, principal lines are marked at the beginning with H (for *Hauptstimme*), and at the end with a right-angled bracket.

harmonic (harm.). A flute-like sound (produced on a string instrument by lightly touching the string with the finger instead of pressing it down).

hörbar. Audible.

immer. Always, continually.

jeté. With a bouncing motion of the bow.

jusqu'à la fin. To the end.

kaum. Hardly, barely.

langsam. Slow.

langsamer. Slower.

langueur. Languor.

largamente. Broadly.

larghetto. Slightly faster than largo.

largo. A very slow tempo.

languente. Languishing.

lassen. Leave, allow.

lebhaft. Lively.

legatissimo. A more forceful indication of *legato.*

legato. Performed without any perceptible interruption between notes.

légèrement. Lightly.

leggiero (legg.). Light and graceful.

legno. The wood of the bow (*col legno tratto,* bowed with the wood; *col legno battuto,* tapped with the wood).

leicht. Light, lightly.

leise. Softly.

lent. Slowly.

lentamente. Slowly.

lento. A slow tempo (between andante and largo).

l.h. Abbreviation for "left hand."

lieblich. Lovely, sweetly.

loco. Indicates a return to the written pitch, following a passage played an octave higher or lower than written.

lontano. Far away, from a distance.

lunga. Long, sustained.

lungo silenzio. A long pause.

ma. But.

marziale. Martial.

mässig. Moderate.

manual. A keyboard played with the

hands (as distinct from the pedal keyboard on an organ).

marcatissimo. With very marked emphasis.

marcato (marc.). Marked, with emphasis.

marcia. March.

marqué. Marked, with emphasis.

même. Same.

meno. Less.

mezza voce. With half the voice power.

mezzo forte (mf). Moderately loud.

mezzo piano (mp). Moderately soft.

mit (m.). With.

M. M. Metronome; followed by an indication of the setting for the correct tempo.

modéré. At a moderate tempo.

modo ordinario (ordin.). In the usual way (usually cancelling an instruction to play using some special technique).

molto. Very, much.

morendo. Dying away.

mormorato. Murmured.

mosso. Rapid.

moto. Motion.

mouvement (mouvt.). Tempo.

muta. Change the tuning of the instrument as specified.

N⌐. In the Schoenberg work, secondary lines are marked at the beginning with N⌐ (for *Nebenstimme*), and at the end with a right-angled bracket.

nachgebend. Becoming slower.

nach und nach. More and more.

naturalezza. A natural, unaffected manner.

naturel. In the usual way, (generally cancelling an instruction to play using some special technique).

nicht. Not.

non. Not.

octava (8va). Octave; if not otherwise qualified, means the notes marked should be played an octave higher than written.

octava bassa (8va. bassa). Play an octave lower than written.

ohne. Without.

open. (1) In brass instruments, the opposite of muted; (2) in string instruments, refers to the unstopped string (i.e. sounding at its full length).

ordinario (ordin.) In the usual way (generally cancelling an instruction to play using some special technique).

ossia. An alternative (usually easier) version of a passage.

ôtez vite les sourdines, Remove the mutes quickly.

parlante. Sung in a manner resembling speech.

Paukenschlägel. Timpani stick.

pedal (ped., P.) (1) In piano music, indicates that the damper pedal should be depressed; an asterisk indicates the point of release (brackets below the music are also used to indicate pedalling) (2) On an organ, the pedals are a keyboard played with the feet.

perdendosi. Gradually dying away.

pesante. Heavily.

peu. Little, a little.

pianissimo (pp). Very soft (*ppp* indicates a still softer dynamic).

piano (p). Soft.

più. More.

pizzicato (pizz.). The string plucked with the finger.

plus. More.

pochissimo (pochiss.). Very little, a very little.

poco. Little, a little.

poco a poco. Little by little.

pomposo. Pompous, majestic, dignified.

ponticello (pont.). The bridge (of a string instrument).

portando la voce. With a smooth sliding of the voice from one tone to the next.

position naturel (pos. nat.). In the normal position (usually cancelling an instruction to play using some special technique).

praeludium. Prelude.

premier mouvement (1er mouvt.). At the original tempo.

préparez le ton. Prepare the instrument to play in the key named.

presto. A very quick tempo (faster than allegro).

principale (pr.) Principal, solo.

punta d'arco. Played with the top of the bow.

quasi. Almost.

quasi niente. Almost nothing, i.e. as softly as possible.

quasi trill (tr.). In the manner of a trill.

quintus. An older designation for the fifth part in a vocal work.

rallentando (rall., rallent.). Growing slower.

recitative (recit.). A vocal style designed to imitate and emphasize the natural inflections of speech.

retenu. Held back.

rigore di tempo. Strictness of tempo.

ritardando (rit., ritard.) Gradually slackening in speed.

ritenuto. Immediate reduction of speed.

rubato. A certain elasticity and flexibility of tempo, consisting of slight accelerandos and ritardandos according to the requirements of the musical expression.

ruhig. Quietly.

rullante. Rolling.

sans timbre. Without snares.

scena vuota. Empty stage.

scherzando (scherz.). Playful.

schmachtend. Languishing.

schnell. Fast.

schneller. Faster.

secco. Dry, simple.

seconda volta. The second time.

segue. (1) Continue to the next movement without pausing; (2) continue in the same manner.

sehr. Very.

semplicità. Simplicity.

sempre. Always, continually.

sensibile. Sensitive.

senza. Without.

sforzando, sforzato (sfz, sf). With sudden emphasis.

sfumato. Diminishing and fading away.

simile. In a similar manner.

sino al. Up to the . . . (usually followed by a new tempo marking, or by a dotted line indicating a terminal point).

smorzando (smorz.). Dying away.

solo (s.). Executed by one performer.

sonator. Player (*uno sonator,* one player; *due sonatori,* two players).

soprano (s.). The voice classification with the highest range.

sordino (sord.). Mute.

sostenendo, sostenuto. Sustained.

sotto voce. In an undertone, subdued, under the breath.

sourdine. Mute.

soutenu. Sustained.

spiccato. With a light bouncing motion of the bow.

staccatissimo. Very staccato.

staccato (stacc.) Detached, separated, abruptly disconnected.

stentando, stentato (stent.). Delaying, retarding.

stesso movimento. The same basic pace.

stretto. In a non-fugal composition, indicates a concluding section at an increased speed.

stringendo (string.). Quickening.

subito (sub.). Suddenly, immediately.

sul. On the (as in *sul G,* on the G string).

suono. Sound, tone.

sur. On.

tacet. The instrument or vocal part so marked is silent.

tanto. Too much.

tasto solo. In a continuo part, this indicates that only the string instrument plays; the chord-playing instrument is silent.

tempo primo (tempo I, Imo.). At the original tempo.

tenor, tenore (T.). The highest male voice.

tenuto (ten.). Held, sustained.

tiefe. Deep, low-pitched.

tornando al tempo primo. Returning to the original tempo.

touch. Fingerboard (of a string instrument).

toujours. Always, continually.

tranquillo. Quietly, calmly.

tre corda (t.c.) Release the soft (or *una corda*) pedal of the piano.

tremolo (trem). On string instruments, a quick reiteration of the same tone, produced by a rapid up-and-down movement of the bow; also a rapid alternation between two different notes.

très. Very.

trill (tr.) The rapid alternation of a given note with the diatonic second above it. In a drum part it indicates rapid alternating strokes with two drumsticks.

troppo. Too much.

tutti. Literally, "all"; usually means all the instruments in a given category as distinct from a solo part.

una corda (u.c.). With the "soft" pedal of the piano depressed.

unison (unis.). The same notes or melody played by several instruments at the same pitch. Often used to emphasize that a phrase is not to be divided among several players.

verkingend. Fading away.

vibrato. On string instruments, a wavering of the pitch, produced by a rapid vibration of the finger stopping the string.

viel, viele. Many.

vivace. Quick, lively.

vivo. Lively.

voce. Voice (as in *colla voce,* a direction for the accompaniment to follow the solo part in tempo and expression).

wie ein Hauch. Like a breath.

wie oben. As above, as before.

wüthend. Furiously.

zart. Tenderly, delicately.

Zeit. Time.

Zeitmass. Tempo.

zögernd. Lingering, retarding.

zu. The phrases *zu 2, zu 3* (etc.) indicate that the part is to be played in unison by 2, 3 (etc.) players.

zurückhaltend. Slackening in speed.

Index of Forms and Genres

A roman numeral following a title indicates a movement within the work named.